THE UNDATABLE GAY COMES AGAIN

MARK DAVID WOOLLARD

SPELLBOUND BOOKS

First Published by in 2024 by SpellBound Books

For my Mum and Dad

Who have always let me be me.

Who have always supported me.

And who have loved me unconditionally

PREVIOUSLY ON THE UNDATEABLE GAY...

Hello! It's me again. Mark Morgan. And no, I'm still no relation to Piers. I praise the Lord every day for that mercy.

If anybody cares, I'm still single and without a man to call my own. I sometimes ponder whether my destiny is to spend a life in my own company, with nothing but the occasional one night stand and a glass of Savvy B to keep me lubricated.

Well, I say occasional one night stand. I use that word occasionally tentatively. I like sex. So shoot me. And as a single gay man, I have needs that NEED to be fulfilled. There's only so many times that giving yourself a hand shandy whilst watching Porn Hub will suffice!

But if I am to endure a lonely life with no gentleman by my side, I have one fear. Dying alone. Which is why I make sure I spend plenty of time with my three nephews, spoiling them. Obviously I do this because I love them unconditionally, but also in the vain hope they will remember my loving deeds when it comes to my latter years. In a time when I'm shitting my Y-fronts or laying in my own piss, in dire need of a bed bath. What a future for those three boys!

My current Grindr profile has changed somewhat since the last time I revealed it. And I've streamlined it:

MARK FUCK-A-LOT

If you lick my balls, I'll be yours forever.

Simple and to the point. It smacks of desperation I know, but if the cap fits… This reminds me of a time when I believed that that saying was 'if the CAT fits'. I remember the first time I made the mistake and Tullene looking at me in bewilderment. But yes, I know that's how she looks at me most of the time anyway.

Tullene, in case you need reminding, is my best friend who has suffered and laughed with me since we were sweet sixteen.

"CAT?!?" Tullene questioned.

"Yes. If the cat fits."

"Fits where?"

"Through the catflap, I'm sure that's the saying."

She looked at me inquisitively. And also shot me a look as if to say, I'm sure you must have been dropped on your head when you were a baby.

Obviously with age and wisdom, well, I don't know quite how much wisdom, I've learnt that the old adage is about baseball caps and not cats.

Now, if you cast your mind back, I last left you on New Year's day 2018 and I'd just woken up to a drunken voicemail from Travis.

He was declaring his undying love for me. For anybody with early onset dementia (or people who just have better things to remember), Travis is a boy I met back in 2002, in a nightclub in Soho, that is long since gone. And he has kept popping up like the proverbial bad penny ever since. There's been chance meetings at the most inappropriate moments, but for some reason, the universe has never quite aligned our love chakras.

Until that cold New Year's Day morning in 2018, that is. When he finally decided to take the plunge and confess how he truly felt for me via a voicemail.

Oh, and in case it had also slipped your mind, I'd joined a gay walking group. And there was a man in said group, who had caught my eye, Billy.

It's getting silly all this.

CHAPTER 1

Batty Boy- Please don't do that (February 2018)

Barry was a man who I found very attractive. Who am I kidding? I find most men attractive. I often joke if they've got a pulse and a cock, they've got a chance. Although, the pulse isn't always a pre-requisite. That's a joke before anybody accuses me of being a necrophiliac.

Barry was a client who I'd massaged a few times and we had quite a flirty relationship. I thought he fancied me and wanted more than just a massage. Boy, how wrong could I have been?

As I effleuraged his thigh, that's industry speak for a long sweeping stroke, I noticed his legs open slightly and I could have sworn he had an erection. My hand went to effleurage more than just his thigh, but I thought better of it.

I continued professionally in the job for which I was being paid and noticed his legs spread further apart. He obviously wants a happy ending; that was the thought process going through my brain. So I took my opportunity and slipped my hand up his Dolce Gabbana boxers.

My eyes widened as he knocked my hand from his semi erect penis.

"Please don't do that!"

OH. MY. GOD. Ground swallow me now. I'd come to the realisation that in this situation, the ground was going to be the only thing that was likely to be doing any swallowing.

"I'm so sorry. I thought you wanted it. I read the situation very wrong."

Blushing, mortified, I finished his massage and hurriedly packed up my couch. I couldn't have gotten out of his flat quicker had I been chased by naked ladies flashing their vaginas at me.

"Tullene!"

"Oh god. What's happened now?" came her response.

Of course, the first thing I was going to do was phone Tullene during the dilemma of accidentally touching up my fit client.

"Why the hell did you do it?"

"I just… I don't know. I read the signals wrong."

"Did he pay you?" she enquired.

"No."

"I don't blame him."

Mortified, red faced, flushed, I got into my car. I couldn't get home fast enough. I needed a large glass of plonk to get over the shock of my wrong move.

As I was driving along the A316, a road that takes you out of Central London, I noticed an HGV lorry driving rather close to my bumper, flashing his headlights.

"If he gets any closer, I'll have to start charging rent!" Yes, I do talk to myself on a regular basis.

I wound down my window. Well, I say wound down, I've got automatic windows so all I actually did was press a button and hey presto.

I did a two finger salute out of the automatically wound down window and called him a prick.

No one gets that close to my back entrance without me seeing a face pic first. And I certainly couldn't see him in my rear view mirror as it was rather dark.

We pulled up at a red traffic light and he approached on my left hand side. I could see him shouting something out of my peripheral.

I pressed the button on my passenger side window. Automatic as well you know.

"Sorry?" I screamed.

"Why are you sticking your fingers up at me?" He was a rather butch looking man but I refused to feel threatened by his masculinity.

"Why are you flashing your headlights at me?" I retorted.

He obviously noticed I was a bit light in my loafers. He kissed his lips, rude boy style.

"Batty boy. That's what you are!"

The traffic lights changed to green and my mouth dropped open. It's not often I'm rendered speechless. His HGV sped off in front of me and it took a second to compose myself. But I'd still managed to take down his number plate, even though his words had floored me.

I'd been homophobically abused at a set of traffic lights in Richmond. I pressed the call button on my car phone and Siri asked, "how can I help you?".

"CALL TULLENE!"

CHAPTER 2

Front Page News (24 hours after Batty boy road rage-gate)

After being homophobically abused in broad daylight. Well, okay, it was the evening so it was actually rather dark, but you catch my drift. I rushed home and did what any reputable gay boy would do in similar circumstances. I opened the fridge and reached for the nearest ice cold bottle of Savvy B that I could get my limp wrists on.

Pouring an extra-large glass, I paced the lounge. I was feeling so many emotions. Shock. Sadness. Sadness that we still live in a world where this could happen. And anger. Anger was the dominating feeling. Something had to be done about this driver of the HGV lorry. Having taken down his particulars, well, number plate, I discovered the company he worked for. And the hand not holding my freezing cold glass of New Zealand beverage picked up my phone and I took to Twitter.

I HAVE JUST BEEN VERBALLY AND HOMOPHOBICALLY ABUSED BY ONE OF YOUR DELIVERY DRIVERS. HE CALLED ME A BATTY BOY. PLEASE RETWEET AND SHARE EVERYBODY

And before I had even finished my first glass of Savvy B, hundreds of people had retweeted and shared it. Be careful what you wish for.

And amongst the retweeters were half of the daily tabloids. And before I could say batty boy, my inbox was full of messages from journalists wanting an interview. Had I created a monster?

Wearing a hole in the beige floor covering, AKA the carpet, I paced some more and grappled for the bottle to pour myself a second large glass.

Giving myself a metaphorical slap, I decided I should reply to the journalists. Why should this man be allowed to get away with this behaviour? I had to make an example of him to protect any weaker, vulnerable homosexuals from having to live through the same experience. So I clicked open my Twitter messages and started replying…

Having finished a bottle (or two) of my favourite tipple, I awoke with a start. Dazed, I picked up my phone to check the time. 08:43. And SIX missed calls from Tullene. SIX? Even by her standards, that's a lot so I quickly hit redial.

"MARK!"

"Don't shout. My head is delicate."

"Have you seen the papers this morning?"

"Who even buys a paper anymore?" I quipped.

"Don't be pedantic!" She'd swallowed a dictionary as well as reading the newspapers. "You're all over the front covers of most of the tabloids!"

Now, anyone who knows Tullene, knows that she has a reputation for elaborating the reality of a situation. But this early morning revelation from her certainly earned a reaction from me and I shot up in my bed.

"What are you talking about?"

And before you could holler, READ ALL ABOUT IT, I clicked on the headlines on my iPhone, and for once, I wished this was all a figment of Tullene's imagination. But alas no, my face was staring back at me on the front cover of The Mirror.

DELIVERY DRIVER CALLED GAY MASSAGE THERAPIST BATTY BOY FROM VAN DURING HOMOPHOBIC ROAD RAGE ROW

The headline says it all, I thought. What a way to get over your hangover. Being splashed all over the front covers of the daily's. That sure woke me up with a start.

Through blurry Savvy B hungover eyes, I managed to read the rest of the article.

THE FIRM IS "URGENTLY INVESTIGATING" AFTER MARK MORGAN CLAIMS HE WAS ABUSED BY AN AGGRESSIVE DELIVERY MAN IN WHAT HE HAS CALLED A "HATE CRIME"

It's not a fucking claim, I screamed internally.

THE HOMOPHOBIC SLUR WAS ALLEGDELY DIRECTED AT MARK MORGAN DURING A ROAD RAGE INCIDENT.

Not bloody allegedly, I took a sharp intake of breath through my nostrils. And then I got to the bit where they quoted part of my tweet, word for word.

I CAN COPE WITH ROAD RAGE, THAT'S FINE. BUT DON'T BRING SEXUALITY, COLOUR OR WHATEVER INTO IT. HE WAS A NASTY, NASTY MAN. I DEFINITELY THINK HE SHOULD BE SACKED.

The article finished with:

A SPOKESMAN FOR THE FIRM SAID, "ABUSIVE LANGUAGE AND BEHAVIOUR HAS ABSOLUTELY NO PLACE WITHIN OUR BUSINESS. WE ARE URGENTLY INVESTIGATING AND WE WILL TAKE THE APPROPRIATE ACTION."

Well, I was wide awake by the end of that news story. .

Another missed call from Tullene.

"Tullene?"

"The whole of my office have seen you in the papers."

"Do you think I can leave my flat? What if the paparazzi are waiting for me?"

Tullene belly laughed down the phone but it was a genuine concern.

INCOMING CALL: MUM

"My mum's calling. I've gotta go."

"She's probably seen you on the news."

I clicked to end the call. Taking a sharp intake of breath; I knew I was going to need that before answering the call to Mummy Morgan.

"Hello?"

"As soon as I opened my iPad this morning, what do I see? Your HD eyebrows staring back at me with some headline calling you a baking boy."

"Batty boy mum."

"That's what I said."

Whipping me into a frenzy, Mother Morgan had some harsh words for me.

"I'm scared of you going out. The papers have made you a target for gay bashers."

CHAPTER 3

Sorry, I don't like it (That night)

I needed a distraction from the media frenzy that had been created. So what better way than to open my Grindr? It didn't take long for a Romanian boy to pop up, PARDON THE PUN, in my inbox.

"You want come round?"

He didn't need to ask me twice. This is what I love about Grindr. It's like Uber for sex.

Arriving at his front door, I hardly had time to take my shoes off. Before I could say kiss me quick, he had passionately lip locked me up against his eggshell painted walls. YES, EGGSHELL. Before I started overthinking his décor choices, I decided now wasn't the time to question which decade I was in.

He wasted no time in slipping his hand down my jogging bottoms. Yes, I was wearing jogging bottoms. Get over it. What can I say? I'm a self-professed gay chav.

After a rather long time fondling my penis, he took his hand out, pushed me away and removed his lips from mine.

"Sorry, I don't like it." And I had to leave.

CHAPTER 4

Let me introduce you to my Buttplug (48 hours after Batty boy road rage-gate. And twenty four hours after being told by a Romanian that he didn't like my penis.)

And no, I'm not talking about my sex aid. Buttplug is the nickname I affectionately call my darling mate Sarah who was unfortunate to meet me in my school days, back in 1989. Hence, my longest serving friend. And we've been buddies ever since.

Now, I know a lot of you will be questioning how she came to have such an attractive nickname. Well, unfortunately it's not as interesting at it appears. Her surname is Butler and in my immature, down in the gutter mind, BUTTPLUG was born.

But that's not to say that I haven't exaggerated how she happened to come by such a pet name over the years. When I meet a new boyfriend of hers, I often let slip "Buttplug" when talking to her, in the vain hope said new boyfriend will question such a name. Although she always threatens me before such meetings. "My name is SARAH tonight, NOT Buttplug." But these warnings always fall on deaf ears.

"Buttplug? That's an interesting nickname…" her most recent rendezvous enquired.

I was more than willing to fill him in.

"Well, it's because when we were at university, we caught her pleasuring herself with a buttplug." Yes, I'm a bastard.

Waiting for the train to Waterloo, I saw an incoming call from Buttplug. I was on my way to meet her for drinks in Soho.

"BUTTPLUG!" I bellowed down the phone.

"I've got you on speaker. Can you not?"

"How long have you known me? And you still risk putting me on speaker phone?"

"Fair point. I've got no-one to blame but myself."

"Is your mum still scared you're going to be gay bashed and fed to wild wolves?"

"She was telling me to be careful. She even made me promise to wear sunglasses to stop me from being recognised."

"It's FEBRUARY! I think you'll be even more conspicuous with them on."

That was a rather big word for her, although she is one of my more intellectual friends.

"Have you met my mum?" She has, many times since 1989. "She's made me paranoid. I'm scared to be out in public."

"Don't panic! You'll be with me in Soho soon. I'll look after you."

Putting the phone down, actually, why do I still say putting the phone down? You can tell I'm an 80's baby who grew up with a rotary dial telephone complete with a cord, that you did actually have to put down. I'll rephrase that; as I ended the call, a woman grabbed my arm. She looked like a lesbian.

"Sorry, I couldn't help overhearing. Are you going through a stressful situation? Let me stay with you until you get on the train safely. It always worries me when I hear someone in distress on a station platform. I worry they might throw themselves in front of the next train."

Not feeling suicidal in the slightest, but to be polite, I let the woman escort me onto the train. And when I say escort, she kept me half a mile back from the yellow line and she gripped onto my arm tight as we stepped onto the train together.

Finally in Soho, I hugged my Buttplug and she placed a glass of Savvy B in my hand. She knows me so well.

"You can take the shades off now."

Checking over my shoulder for any undercover journalists

"Are you sure? I've had to dodge the paps." Oh how we laughed. The quote of the night everytime someone looked at me was, "Yes, yes, it is me!" as though they'd recognised me from the newspapers.

Tucking into a fillet steak in the Soho branch of The Ivy, I noticed a couple stop in the window to stare at me and Buttplug as we were stuffing our faces. I looked up and stared them straight in the eye. Deadpan, I held my hand up and went "Yes. Yes, it is me!" Buttplug collapsed from her chair in fits of giggles as she noticed they were actually checking out the menu which happened to be above my head in the front window. That was awkward.

Shovelling the last of our dessert into our gob holes, I grabbed the waiter and asked for the bill.

"You're keen to get out of here", my dinner partner commented.

"I need to get into G-A-Y bar. I need a stiff drink and a dance after the last couple of days."

Paying the bill, we grabbed our coats and went to exit the brasserie. I felt a tap on my shoulder. Thinking it was Buttplug trying to wind me up, I ignored the tapping. And then I heard a man's voice boom from behind me.

"Excuse me young man!"

That's not Sarah's voice, I thought. Not unless someone slipped testosterone pills in her peppercorn sauce. We both turned around and I smiled sweetly, expecting it to be one of my fans who had seen my splashed across the tabloids.

"Yes?" I enquired.

"Sorry to disturb you just as you're walking out…" he began but I didn't give him time to finish.

"Yes. Yes, it is me!" I declared.

Looking bemused, the man looked over at his wife. Well, I assume it was his wife. Although it could have been his mistress for all I knew.

"I'm sorry but my wife really likes your friend's hair shade and was wondering if she could possibly ask her which brand of colour she uses."

"Oh!" I squirmed awkwardly as Buttplug beamed over towards the wife to show her appreciation of the compliment of her hair. I went as red as the lobster that was just being delivered to an adjacent table.

Walking into G-A-Y bar, my so called friend failed to stop mocking me at the mistaken identity.

"Yes. Yes, it is me", she imitated as we strolled up to the bar. Well, I say strolled. I practically sprinted, I was so desperate for a liquid refreshment.

"Oh fuck off!" I pursed my lips as I knocked back a Savvy B that I almost took the barman's arm off to get my hands on.

A few hours of rocking our moves on the dancefloor, I could see Buttplug starting to sway from the effects of the booze. She's on the turn, I thought to myself. I can always tell when she's had too much of the old sauce and it's time to get her home.

So I dragged her from the bar and jumped in a taxi. Well, I jumped. Getting her into it was more of a push. Collapsed on my lap, she left me to make conversation with our uber driver. I mean, I won't lie, I was rather sozzled myself so when the cab driver suddenly started shouting, it gave me a fright.

"YOUR MATE HAS THROWN UP!"

And before you could say, pass us the bucket, I found myself cleaning up her vomit with baby wipes, on the orders of our driver at three o'clock in the morning. Now, that's true friendship.

And then I recalled her words just a few hours earlier on the phone.

"I'll look after you!" Oh yes, you did a good job of that I thought as I scrubbed my hands with Dettol to remove the smell of regurgitated fillet steak from my fingers.

CHAPTER 5

What's your name by the way? (March 2018)

I remember Andy well. I say well. At the time of actual intercourse, I didn't do particularly well at remembering who he was.

I'd just finished leading my gays on a walk in the Surrey Hills and I found myself particularly horny. I find a bit of fresh Surrey countryside air will do that to me. So I loaded my trusted app, Grindr.

This rather handsome man with long ginger hair popped up and asked me if I was free to pop over. Like a bullet from a gun, I was at his flat in a shot and found my barrel inside him.

Just as I was about to cum, a realisation dawned on me. I didn't actually ask what his parents had christened him.

Stopping my thrusting for a split second, I stared him dead in the eye and asked, "What's your name by the way?"

CHAPTER 6

The elephant in the room (A few days later)

Almost four months had gone by since that drunken voicemail from Travis. The so called proverbial bad penny. I hadn't even bothered to contact him again as I was sick of feeling like he had me dangling on the edge of a hook. Until I suddenly received a WhatsApp message. I saw Travis pop up in my inbox.

TRAVIS: I've always felt drawn to you. And now you look more handsome than ever.

I was starting to lose the will to live. You told me I looked handsome on New Year's Eve and you still haven't acted on it. So why are you telling me again? I like action! I'm a great believer that if someone wants you, they will make it their mission to make it happen. But I can't deny, after almost twenty years of Travis popping in and out of my life, there was a pull to him that I just couldn't ignore. I decided a blunt, no nonsense message was called for.

ME: I wish you would damn well act on it…

And then the next message from the elephant himself.

TRAVIS: I will maybe surprise you unexpectedly one day very soon. I can't explain it right now but things have changed very positively for me and I feel as though I can now move on…

Tapping my finger on my phone screen with a little frustration, I wanted to type 'Why can't you just grow some balls and ask me out?' But what I actually typed was…

ME: I shall be waiting for this surprise. I think we deserve a happy ending. It's been three months and 18 days since that drunken voicemail…

And then no reply. Well, not until a few months later anyway.

CHAPTER 7

UBERGATE- my fling with a taxi driver who gave me more than just a ride home (July 2018)

I remember Ahmed as though it were only yesterday. Although how can I not? It's not every day you book an Uber, enter the taxi and then have your driver mistake your penis for their gearstick.

I had just left my nephew's third birthday party and I was feeling rather merry. Well, I say merry. Quite pissed would be more of an accurate description. Some people might question or raise their eyebrows at how one can get so drunk at a three year old's party. I would tell said people to SOD OFF. This is the Morgan family we're talking about.

As I stumbled out of my brother's front door, grasping onto my phone, I struggled to focus my eyes to see the number plate of the car waiting to take me home. Mummy Morgan never ceases to amaze me as she always gives out warnings everytime I catch an Uber.

"You never know who's in that car you're getting into. I brought you all up not to talk to strangers or take lifts from them!"

"MUM! You gave us that warning when we were kids. I'm nearly middle aged!"

OH SHIT! I can't believe I've just realised I'm almost middle aged. If it wasn't for the fact I'm stabbed up with so much botox, my face may have dropped from the shock of the realisation.

"You mark my words, Mark! You never stop being a parent, no matter how old your kids are. You just wait and see once you've got your own!"

"I don't intend to find out mother. Ankle biters!"

"Big mistake dear. Whose going to wipe your arse when you start shitting yourself? Why do you think I had you kids?"

NICE! Nice to know why my parents really wanted to bring me into this world. A ready-made carer for their old age.

Mummy Morgan's midnight warnings echoing in my ears were disturbed by a bright set of headlights dazzling me. Closing one eye, thinking it would help me focus on the licence plate better, I managed to read HX68 LWO. *Ahmed had arrived.* My optician would be proud of me.

Attempting to enter the car in as sober state as I could muster, I gripped the door handle and MISSED twice before I managed to win the battle of opening the passenger side door. *NOW, sit down elegantly with poise,* I told myself. At which point, my left foot got caught on the seatbelt and I smash landed into the seat, my hand landing on Ahmed's knee.

"OH MY GOD!", I screamed, forgetting to actually remove said hand from said knee, "I'M SORRY!" I don't know why but I was speaking so loudly; some might even refer to it as screaming.

AWKWARD SILENCE. And then Ahmed looked at my hand which was still rested on his knee cap. And then he looked up at me. I smiled awkwardly. And then he looked back down at his knee once more. And then I looked down at his knee, hand seemingly frozen to the spot. I garnered some speed and flapped my hand away.

Flustered, flapping and floundering; That's a nice bit of alliteration. That creative writing course I once took wasn't a complete waste of time after all. Anyway, flustered, flapping and floundering, I attempted to reach for the seatbelt and eventually winning the fight, I clicked it into place. Another awkward silence ensued as I noticed Ahmed hadn't driven away yet. My eyes widening, I wondered whether I should point out his lack of acceleration on the pedal.

"Can you shut door please?" I detected a strong Egyptian accent. Well, truth be told, I wouldn't know an Egyptian accent if it came up and slapped me round the face with a camel. But he was dark, handsome and mysterious.

"OH HOLY SHIT BALLS!" I bellowed. No wonder we hadn't set off on our journey yet. He was waiting for me to close the door. WHOOPS.

"You pissed?"

Why do drunk people always pretend to be sober when we're quite clearly intoxicated?

"No. Just had maybe one or two glasses of vino at my nephew's birthday party."

"Is his 18th?"

THIS IS AWKWARD.

"No. Three years old today."

Ahmed raised his eyebrows. He clearly hasn't had botox, I noticed. But I did clock that the eyebrows were rather black and extremely bushy so it was a very noticeable raise. I could see sheer judgment on his face for being boozed up at a kid's party. *BOLLOCKS TO HIM. I SHALL IGNORE HIM FOR THE REST OF THE TRIP HOME.*

"You very handsome boy."

My ignorance didn't last long. Feeling a Savvy B daze coming over me, I had to double check Ahmed was actually talking to me. I mean, I don't know who else I thought he may be chatting to considering I was the only other person in the car. Flashing me a smile of his dazzling white teeth, it was an affirmative. He was calling ME handsome. He wasn't too shabby looking himself but being the coy gay boy that I am, I had to play hard to get.

"Thank you", I blushed. Well, as much as one can blush through a couple of layers of fake tan and a splash MAC foundation.

And then quite unexpectedly, I felt a hand on my gearstick. Sorry, I mean penis. My bright blue eyes nearly popping out of their sockets, I assumed Ahmed had mistaken it for the car's joystick and suddenly misjudged the positioning of his car's instruments. I can't blame him, after all- it's an easy mistake to make with the size of my man meat.

OKAY- who am I kidding? I know I was at the back of the queue when God was handing out the monster cocks. But even so, I've never had any complaints. Well, apart from this one time that some cunt asked me if he could borrow my penis to floss his teeth. But I can't talk about that night right now; it's triggering me.

Realising we were on a dual carriageway and travelling at a constant 50mph, it dawned on me that Ahmed didn't need to perform a gear change. So the fact his hand seemed to be strategically placed on my crown jewels was quickly becoming apparent to be no accident.

"You getting hard?", he grinned. You couldn't fool him. He knew an erection when he felt one.

And then it was my turn to change his gear and his was already in fifth gear, if you catch my drift. Smiling, he pulled into a lay-by and leaning over, he kissed me. That's very forward, I thought. And then I reminded myself that minutes earlier he'd randomly placed his hand on my gearstick so formalities were out the window.

Coming up for air, I managed to gasp out the words;

"You better leave me a five star passenger review on my uber profile!"

And then the hazard lights were on and my legs seemed to be spread eagled on the back seat.

CHAPTER 8

Don't try to drown your best friend (September 2018)

"Let's go to Marbella!" screamed Buttplug.

"Only if Tullene can come too!" I screamed back.

"The more, the merrier!" She screamed back.

I don't know why we were screaming but I think it's just second nature to me. I only have one volume and that's LOUD. I'm that friend that you can't risk having on speakerphone. A fact Tullene found out to her peril in Tesco one time. It was soon after Ahmed gave me a ride. Home. In his taxi.

"TULLENE! My Uber driver grabbed my penis. I think he mistook it for his gearstick. And then he fucked…….."

The line went dead. Apparently she was in the self-service queue, full of old ladies with their pink rinses and shopping trolleys. One gasped as she heard my words blaring out of Tullene's apple device. And according to Tullene's story, the lady nearly had a stroke when she heard what I said. And I'm not talking about her having a stroke of the checkout boy's nether regions. Tullene took the decisive action of ending the call before she became responsible for a death in the supermarket queue.

Before you could shout "SANGRIA!", we were arriving at Gatwick airport, getting ready to fly on EasyJet. Yes, EasyJet. Not my airline of choice. What can I say? I'm a British Airways snob. Although, I must confess, I'm not so keen on them since they've stopped selling M&S food onboard. And yes, before anybody else pipes up, I'm a Marks and Spencer snob too.

Now, for anyone who is familiar with Tullene, you will know that she's not been genetically blessed in the health department. Bless her little heart. She's got numerous medical conditions, one of which is sleep apnoea. She has to wear a mask to sleep in at night. A CPAP machine, to be exact- there's a bit of medical knowledge for you. Who says my ramblings aren't educational?! I do like to make sure readers of my diaries learn something. I'm nice like that.

Anyhow, I've wandered off the beaten track here, distracted by thoughts of Tullene's attractive night-time sleep aids- although it's more than just an aid. If she doesn't have it, she could die. But that fact doesn't stop me taking the piss out of her for having it. When we go away, we often share a bed, like most best friends do, I'm sure. And before she had this machine, she was the most god awful snorer. I could have smothered her most nights. But luckily, her mask has put paid to her snoring so I can actually sleep with her now, without murderous thoughts of throttling her.

And because of numerous health conditions, she also has a number of pills to keep her alive too. She once offered to be a surrogate mother for me should I ever wish to have children. But I politely declined.

"Not being rude Tullene. It's a really kind gesture but I'm not sure you've got the best genes to pass on."

We arrived at check in, Tullene with her two suitcases. YES, TWO. She always has to buy extra luggage anytime we fly, just to make sure she has enough space for all her medication. I call it her pharmacy case.

Does anybody else always get nervous at airports until they get through airport security? I do. I don't know why. It's one of my irrational fears. I know I'm no drugs baron but that doesn't stop me panicking that someone may have planted cocaine in my suitcase. I've got an overactive imagination, I know.

Once strapped into our aeroplane seats, safely through security having not been arrested for being dope peddlers, the cabin crew got Savvy B flowing for us. I've been bought up in the belief that it's rude not to have a drink at an airport or on a flight. Sarah, AKA Buttplug, isn't really a big drinker, I mean, not that you'd know it after vomiting in the taxi-gate. But every now and again, she does indulge and she's normally safest on Vodka.

As she took a sip of her V&T, I looked her straight in the eye, deadpan.

"Now go easy Butt, I'm not cleaning up puke from an aeroplane seat."

BUTT is what I usually call her when we're out in public. It's safer. And she prefers it. I remember the time she was meeting me at a church fayre and I screamed "BUTTPLUG!" across the field as soon as I clapped eyes on her. She went an interesting shade of crimson. She had to leave early that day after being accused by the elderly cake stall holder of bringing sex toys to a holy event.

Arriving in Marbella, the three of us a little tipsy, we decided our first stop should be the Ocean club. If you've never been, you really should try it. It's basically a massive piss up by a swimming pool but the sights you see there really are for sore eyes. It's great for people watching.

One lady I spotted looked like she'd had her face pulled back by a whole roll of cling film. And as for the men, all muscular with muscles on their muscles and covered in baby oil. And no, I'm not describing a porn film I've recently watched.

And then the dreaded words left both of my holiday companion's mouths.

"Let's go for a swim!" Tullene yelled.

"I'm there!" Echoed Buttplug.

To an outsider, the pastime may seem perfectly harmless and innocent and should bring no dread whatsoever. But Buttplug can barely swim and Tullene can't swim at all. Even with armbands.

"I'm not having you both on my back!" I retorted.

It has been known that I've had to give Tullene a piggy back in the pool before now. Which is no mean feat considering she has been very well blessed in the breast department. Although, some might argue that they'd be handy floatation devices.

Reluctantly I agreed to get into the pool with them.

"Okay, IF we go swimming, we are staying in the shallow end where you can both touch the bottom." FAMOUS LAST WORDS.

Just as the three of us stepped into the pool, a very handsome muscular man with muscles that could walk on their own, caught my eye. And he winked at me. Well, I'm pretty sure it was a wink. He may well have been squinting because the sun was in his eye. But I'm sure it was the former.

"Here", I whispered to the girls. It probably wasn't a whisper as we all know I have trouble with my volume switch. "Don't look now but that man with pecs the size of melons and the six pack like a wash board just winked at me."

Why I was stupid enough to start that sentence with "don't look now" is beyond me. I obviously momentarily forgot who I was holidaying with and gave them more credit than they deserved. Because what did Tullene and Buttplug do? So to avoid embarrassment and to save me from the awkward pretence that we weren't looking over, I just gave him a little coy wave. And he waved back. The girl's indiscretion did me a favour for once.

"Let's get in the pool!" For someone who has the swimming capability of a newborn baby, Tullene is always very eager to get in the water.

"But I've pulled!" I protested.

"He'll still be here after we've had a dip!"

And before you could say paddle, I was in the pool with two inadequate swimmers.

Buttplug, being slightly more sensible than Tullene, stayed within paddling depth. But oh no, not Tullene. She decided that she would cling onto my back as I swam into deeper depths.

Suddenly having a coughing fit, she let go of my back and tried to put her feet to the bottom, forgetting she was out of her depth. I saw her head plop under the water.

I leaped into David Hasselhoff mode and grabbed her by the armpits, which luckily she'd shaved for Marbella, and pulled her up. By this point she was panicking, and she put her hands on my perfectly pruned spiky hair to give her some floatation and my head went under.

"MY HAIR!" I managed to yell as my head plunged under.

For anybody who knows me well, my hair was my pride and joy. I use the word WAS because this incident was before I went bald but that's a story for another time. I always had my GHD's to hand so I could straighten my locks into the perfect spikes. And the amount of hairspray I used to use to freeze them safely into place would have given Greta Thunberg a stroke. What ozone layer?...

Managing to push Tullene's hands from my bonce, I rushed up from underneath the water and gasped for breath.

"TULLENE! I'm trying to save you. Talk about biting the hand that feeds you…………."

I couldn't finish my sentence. She had her hands on my spiky locks once more, shoving my head beneath the pool water.

GREAT. I'd just been flirted with by an Adonis and I'd never get to know how it was to end as my best friend was trying to drown me.

Spluttering, I managed to come up for air once more. I could see from the corner of my watery, bloodshot eye, the said Adonis still looking over in my direction and waving. So I waved back with sheer desperation, signalling I was in danger of death. But alas, he thought it was nothing more than a flirtatious shake of the fingers and raised his glass of wine and mouthed the words, "CHEERS!"

I took the opportunity to scream.

"HELP!"

But no sooner had I screamed, before Tullene had pushed my head back under. Ruining my hair was going to cause me anger enough but if my fake tan and foundation was coming off my face, I'd decided that I would kill her. That's if she hadn't drowned me first.

And then like magic, a rubber ring landed in the pool next to us and Tullene grasped onto it. I came up to the surface like Aerial in "The Little Mermaid", albeit not as glamorous as I was clamouring and gasping for air. And I wasn't singing, *I wanna be where the people are* either as I was currently struggling to breathe, let alone belt out a tune from a Disney film.

The Adonis had saved the day by supplying a rubber ring. And then I decided it was only fair to repay him by supplying him with a ring of my own.

CHAPTER 9

SIMON- the naked masseur (a few days later)

After the PTSD that arises because of your best friend trying to drown you to save herself, I decided I needed… No, not needed. I DESERVED a massage. And not just to soothe the PTSD. Tullene and her mahoosive (that's my sister's word for MASSIVE) flotation devices, AKA, boobs, had actually pulled on my scalenes and sternocleidomastoid. For those of you with little or no anatomical knowledge, that's two of the muscles in your neck.

Out came my iPhone and Mr Google. I don't know why I always assume Google is a man. It's probably just my love of the male species that causes me to label every inanimate object as masculine. Actually is Google classed as an inanimate object? I don't know if it can be as it's a piece of computer software but you know what I mean.

LOCAL MASSAGE THERAPISTS HOME VISITS. And up popped many suggestions for someone who could come and sort out my sternocleidomastoid. That sounds ambiguous and there must be a pun there somewhere but I haven't got the mental capacity to think of it right now.

At the risk of having eggs thrown at me for being sexist, I always prefer a male massage therapist. Not only because I'm a self-confessed man maniac but I generally find they give a stronger, deeper massage. Although, don't get me wrong, I have had some female therapists over the years who have given me a right pummelling.

NIKOLAS, a sporty male masseur who has been doing relaxing Swedish massages for over 20 years. Seems perfect. Then I read on. Just one problem. *I do not have any formal qualifications in massage therapy which my rates reflect.*

NEXT! I scrolled on further. Even though Nikolas might have been easy on the eye, I do like my therapist with a Level 3 Diploma in Massage.

SIMON offers soothing Swedish or deep tissue. Professional massage, straight to your home. Relax and unwind. Leave your aches and pains caused by your best friend trying to drown you behind. OKAY, so it didn't say that last bit. But all my boxes had been ticked once I'd read the whole advert. *ITEC LEVEL 3 QUALIFIED.*

TICK! And before I could say effleurage, a tall dark handsome Mediterranean looking masseur was gracing my doorstep.

Obviously, he wasn't on the doorstep for very long. I did actually open the front door and let him into my flat.

After informing him of my problem areas, I left out the explanation of how I had come to have a pulled sternocleidomastoid, due to a sadistic best friend, I undressed and got face down on his massage couch.

I had my face in his hole. I'm talking about the massage table's head hole for any of you with a dirty mind. Anyway, I was lying there for about a minute and I still hadn't felt his hands on me. I debated looking up but I just felt too zen and decided that he was probably getting himself grounded and in the zone.

When another thirty seconds had passed and he still hadn't touched me yet, I decided to have a sneak peek. Turning my neck (as best as I could mind you, considering I was currently suffering with limited motion after almost being drowned- YES, I am going to keep going on about it), my eyes nearly popped out of their sockets.

I was greeted with a set of rather tanned testicles at my eye level. And a rather delectable looking uncut penis. My eyes, surveying the scenery further, saw a stomach that looked like it had never eaten a carbohydrate in its life and a pair of pecs that would rival the size of Pamela Anderson's tits in her Baywatch heyday days.

Well, I wasn't complaining of course. As long as I get a good massage, I guess it's up to him what he decides to wear as his work uniform. It saves on his laundry bills, I suppose.

Reading the room, Simon could tell I was a little taken aback at his choice of workwear attire.

"You don't mind me being naked, do you? I just find it helps me massage better and I get more movement and range of motion from the body."

"Oh no. I don't mind at all. I mean, I'm naked too, aren't i?"

I don't know why I felt the need to say that. But say it I did.

Rubbing his hands over my neck, I could feel my scalenes and stern-ocleidomastoid loosening and I was gaining a full range of motion once more. Which was very handy when being massaged by a naked masseur. It means you get to rotate your neck and see every part of their anatomy.

"It's time to roll over onto your back", I heard Simon say.

PLEASE DON'T HAVE AN ERECTION. I was praying to the massage gods.

As I turned, my prayers had been answered. Mini Mark was still just that. As floppy as a removable disk used for a computer in the

80's and 90's. And maybe the 00's. But don't quote me on that. I'm not sure if anybody from the 00's will even know what a floppy disc is.

"Are you not enjoying the massage?" Simon enquired. A very odd question, I thought to myself.

"Yes. Oh yes, it's great. I feel much better." I reassured him.

"Oh okay." He sounded confused. "It's just most of my clients normally have an erection by now."

And then it dawned on me. Here I was, thinking I'd booked a professional Level 3 diploma therapist, when in fact, I'd actually booked a voyeuristic naked masseur. Who did happen to have a level 3 diploma at least so it wasn't all bad.

"You can touch my pecs and stomach whilst I massage your arms, if you like."

And of course I did. It would have been rude to refuse.

When you break your ribs on a date (October 2018)

I looked at the calendar on the wall. Yes, I do still own a wall calendar. I know most of us use the diaries on our phones these days but I still like to have a physical calendar. And as you can probably imagine, mine are usually very gay. I currently have a firefighters one where they are all topless or very scantily dressed.

I remember in my teens, I would always have the *sexy soap star* calendar donning my wall, which would have all the topless totty from *HOLLYOAKS*- a very melodramatic British soap opera where no-one can act but the cast are all very easy on the eye.

These were the days before the internet even existed so having said topless calendar was all us gay teens from the late 90's and early 00's had to use for our wanking materials. Apart from my sister's *Smash Hits* or *More* magazines that I would often steal from her so I could look at whoever was the male centrefold for that month. Those pages used to get stuck together on a regular basis…

Anyway, where was I? I've completely digressed into my masturbation nostalgia. Oh yes, I was just looking up at my wall calendar and realised it was almost TEN MONTHS since that drunken voicemail from Travis with the promise of a date and the declaration of undying love. TEN FUCKING MONTHS.

But there I was, still waiting for said date to come to fruition. *BASTARD.* He hadn't even asked me yet, hence my use of the expletive. So instead of waiting around for it to happen, I decided to get back on the horse.

And for any of you not familiar with that saying, I'm not talking about gaining a sudden interest in a hobby of horse riding. I simply mean, it's time to start looking for another man. Travis is clearly not the love of my life.

For a while, I actually thought he might be. I believed it was fate that he kept turning up at random intervals in my life over the course of the last fifteen years or so. This called for a heart to heart with some Savvy B, Tullene and Buttplug.

"But why does he keep showing up if it's not meant to be?" I slurred the question slightly. And no, I'm not becoming a lightweight when it comes to the booze. I'd just had a particularly long day and the wine had maybe gone to my head slightly. Just a little bit. Ooooh, that reminds me of Gina G.

"Not every love story has a happy ending like in the films", Tullene informed me.

"Sometimes these men keep showing up as the universe's way of showing you that there's someone better," Buttplug continued for Tullene.

"And you deserve more than that cunt." Tullene finished. When did these two become such a double act?

"Maybe you should both become psychotherapists. You both have such a way with words."

Tullene stuck a finger up at me in faux annoyance and used her other hand to re-fill our glasses. She's multi skilled like that.

As we swigged a few more glasses, my Grindr pinged. *ADAM, 29. FIT!*

"Here, have a look at him!" I waved my phone screen in front of their eyes.

"Ding Dong!" My drinking partners screamed.

"He wants to go to a water park!" Bemused, the room went silent for a few moments.

"That's an interesting first date", Buttplug offered.

"Fuck it! What have I got to lose?"

Apart from a few more pounds, I thought. I'd never been on a first date which involved wearing swimming trunks. Pushing my nerves aside, I reasoned with myself. *At least this way he can see the goods before he tries them.*

Before I could say wave machine, I found myself in a pair of Hawaiian patterned trunks, a little self-conscious at my non-muscular body on show, being greeted by Adam. Also in a pair of loose fitted trunks. Or so I thought. They were just a pair of Adidas sports shorts which he whipped off to reveal speedos.

My eyes couldn't help but be drawn to the package said speedos were packaging. *That certainly would cost a lot if I sent it via Royal Mail.*

Moving my gaze back up to his face so as not appear like a sexual predator, I got distracted by his V's. He obviously works out, I concluded. Moving my eyes further up, (I will get to his face eventually) my ADHD brain stopped again. This time at his perfectly round nipples. Not too big, not too small.

For those who don't know, I am obsessed with nipples. I don't know why. It's just my thing. If I was straight, I would definitely be a boob man.

Finally arriving at his eyes, I wondered whether a first date in nothing but swimwear was appropriate for a perverted gay boy with ADHD. Too many distractions.

We jumped into the pool and were getting along SWIMMINGLY. Do you like what I did there?

We splashed about, slid down some water slides and frolicked in the wave pool. It was actually super fun. Much better than some of the dates I've been on when I just end up getting sloshed and shagging them.

And Adam was very boisterous. I liked that. That was until he got a bit too boisterous and suddenly, out of nowhere, quite unexpectedly, he picked me up. And that is when I felt his true strength. I was having visions of the BFG, that's the Big Friendly Giant, picking me up in his hand. The way he gripped me. He must have thought I was a dumbbell.

My first thought was, *God, he's fucking strong to pick ME up.*

My second thought was, *If he throws me in and messes up my hair, I'll kill him.*

And my third and overriding thought was, *I'm sure I just heard and felt a rib crack.*

But alas, it was too late to worry about any of that as I suddenly appeared to be under the water. Yes, he'd thrown me in. I found myself screaming.

"YOU BASTARD!"

As I surfaced, I imagined I was channelling my inner Little Mermaid but I fear that was an illusion in my head. In fact, in reality, my spiky hair was as flat as a pancake and the only sounds leaving my gob were groans. Meanwhile, Adam thought his play-time was hilarious.

I pulled myself from the pool and I knew something wasn't right. It hurt to breathe and I had a bad pain in my rib area.

"I think I've done something to me ribs!" I declared to my date. What I should have said was, "I think YOU'VE done something to me ribs!" But I wasn't in any fit state to start playing the blame game.

Before you could say intercostal muscles, Adam had driven me to A&E as he could see I seemed to be in considerable pain. After the investigations at the hospital had finished, I just had to call Tullene.

"Tullene! I've broken my bloody ribs!"

CHAPTER 10

Finally, it's happened to me... Or has it? (November 2018)

If anyone has ever broken their ribs, you will feel my pain. I couldn't get comfortable to sleep because of the ache. And then when I could get comfortable, I couldn't breathe. Because let me tell you, breathing with broken ribs is like nothing I can describe. But I'll try.

I imagine it's comparable to child birth. Obviously I have no idea what bearing a baby or going into labour is like as I am a man with a penis. And no womb. Or vagina for said baby to exit from. But from seeing people on the telly go into labour and all the panting and shortness of breath they seem to have; I feel like that's what it might be like.

Let's put it this way; I was certainly in no fit state to be having sex or doing any strenuous exercise right now. Resting on the couch and the occasional walk was as much movement as the doctor allowed.

Until a WhatsApp massage popped up on my phone and a mixture of shock, anger and bemusement came across me. And the emotions ended up making me jump up to the ceiling. Metaphorically.

TRAVIS. After eleven months since the drunken voicemail, he had finally decided to make contact. I couldn't be sure if it was making me happy or filling me with rage.

I was speechless. It was making my heart flutter but it was also making my blood boil simultaneously at just how long it had actually taken him to make contact. So I decided to play it cool. Simply replying with two heart emojis to show my appreciation.

Blunt and to make a point. I had let this man use me as a carrot and dangle me on his string for far too long.

TRAVIS: I hope to see you very soon.

I wasn't going to hold my breath. Cynical but justifiable emotions on my part.

ME: It's been months since that drunken voicemail.

And then radio silence for TWO DAYS.

"If he texts you again and you reply, I will have you admitted to a psychiatric unit." Tullene can be very threatening when she puts her mind to it.

"If the shoe were on the other foot, I know I would say the same to you. But Tullene, there's something somewhere in me that needs to give this a chance."

"You've given him more chances than I've had hot dinners!"

Cor, I hadn't heard that saying since my Nan was alive.

"How old are you by the way Tullene?" We both laughed. And then I followed up the laughter with a scream. Laughing with broken ribs is no laughing matter. Literally.

TWO DAYS LATER…

TRAVIS: Shall we arrange a date? Someday next week? I was thinking of a few glasses of Savvy B somewhere in Soho.

FUCK A DUCK. I had to screenshot the text and send it to Tullene and Buttplug. Just to ensure I wasn't hallucinating. I couldn't quite believe my eyes.

ME: Well bugger me gently. I just had to sit down and pour a glass of Savvy B to recover from the shock. I can't believe you've finally asked me. So… I'm free Wednesday or Saturday?

TRAVIS: Fabulous darling!! Let's do Wednesday. I will be absolutely ecstatic to see you.

ME: Fabulous my little Thomas the tank engine driver!!! It's a date! I think I'll be as nervous as a kid in hospital being visited by Jimmy Saville.

He's a train driver in case you were wondering why I was referring to him as a children's character.

*TRAVIS: *Laughing emojis* You never fail to make me laugh, which is definitely a good thing. I will count down the days.*

I didn't hear from him again for a few days which was making me slightly paranoid. I thought now that he had finally gotten round to asking me out, we might have had some WhatsApp exchanges.

"Listen", Buttplug demanded, "before we had text messages, you would have to call someone to ask them on a date. And then you probably wouldn't speak to them again until the day of the date. There were no text messages before 2000."

I understood her point but I reminded her that we weren't living in pre-2000, it was currently 2018 with advanced technology. And I also reminded her that she's only two years older than me. Yet she was talking like an old dear. But she is an old soul is Buttplug.

The night before the date, I still hadn't heard a peep from Travis. So I thought it was perfectly acceptable to drop him a message.

ME: What time are you thinking tomorrow darling? 7pm?

TRAVIS: Marky!! How are you my darling? I am still at work and absolutely shattered. They have me running around like a right little bitch at the moment with too much work to do. You are going to hate me and think this is a complete mugging off but I promise you and swear to God that it's the absolute truth…

OH GOD. My stomach dropped. I read on.

TRAVIS: …I've been told I need to cover on-call duties tomorrow as one of my colleagues has gone off sick. I am absolutely fucking LIVID as it's so short notice. I do not want to 'cancel' as I want to see you and set a date. So I'm gutted to ask but could we 'reschedule' to next week instead? I can do Tuesday, Wednesday or Friday. And I really hope you are free to meet me one of them? I'm so sorry for messing you around at such short notice. Xxx

Talk about war and peace. He really went round the houses just to cancel on me. Petrified of Tullene's reaction to the latest development, I bit the bullet and dialled her number. She surprised me.

"Well, just text him back and tell him which day you can do next week."

"But he's cancelling on me." I protested.

"He's not cancelling. He's just rescheduling. And I believe he's genuine otherwise he wouldn't give you a list of other potential dates. He'd just fob you off."

Swallowing my stubbornness and reeling from Tullene's calm stance on the situation, I typed a reply.

ME: Well, this is very annoying but what can you do? But never mind, all good things come to those who wait. We've waited all these years so what difference will one more week make?? How about Tuesday?

TRAVIS: Tuesday works perfectly for me and I shall very much look forward to it. Thank you for being so understanding and accommodating.

CHAPTER 11

You're cute until you open your mouth (a few hours later)

Regardless of Tullene's opinion, I still felt a little hurt by Travis 'rescheduling' our date. So what's a deflated gay boy to do to cheer himself up?

Most people would probably say open a bottle of Savvy B or have a cream cake. But I say, go on Grindr and a find a rendezvous. A tryst. Call it what you will.

Before you could say 'MISTEEQ', not everybody will understand that reference but they sang a very catchy song entitled 'ONE NIGHT STAND'. There's a little nostalgia for all my fellow people who grew up in the 90's and 00's.

Ashley, who had commented I was very cute, turned up on my doorstep. Don't you just love Grindr? Literally the Deliveroo for sex.

"Alright mate!" I was feeling particularly butch as I opened the door and dragged him over the threshold. "I hope you're fucking horny coz I need a good shag."

Ashley, obviously not used to being greeted quite so bluntly, raised an eyebrow. Clearly not had botox with that much movement on his face either, I judged.

"You're cute until you open your mouth." He too showed he could be blunt with his words.

"I'll take that as a compliment." And then I showed him exactly what I could do with my mouth.

CHAPTER 12

I never thought I'd see the day (A week later)

THE NIGHT BEFORE…

TRAVIS: Mr Mark!

ME: Mr Travis!

*ALSO ME: *sends voicemail he left me on NYE as an attachment**

TRAVIS: I do not have the courage to listen to that voice note. I've no doubt it is the voicemail I left you which would be extremely embarrassing on my part.

ME: Yes, I thought you might not be keen to listen to the voicemail you left me. I listen to it often and it makes me laugh so much.

He chose to ignore that part.

TRAVIS: Are you still on for meeting me tomorrow for our date as it seems like it's taken a lifetime to come to fruition?

ME: Oh of course I still want to see you tomorrow. I'm quite looking forward to it. It's going to be very exciting having a catch up and seeing if there's any potential for a future romance.

Was that too keen? Too forward? Too bloody late anyway as I'd already pressed send.

TRAVIS: If we both aim to be outside G-A-Y bar for 7ish, I'd like to think we would naturally find each other? And then we can walk up and get a table somewhere.

How romantic. Naturally find each other, like it's somehow meant to be.

ME: I'm sure we will naturally find each other. We'll sniff each other out.

Not quite as romantic a reply as I was hoping my fingers would type out. Instead I made us sound like a pair of police dogs on the lookout for hard drugs.

TWO HOURS BEFORE…

I was all sixes and sevens. In a right two and eight, I was. I didn't know what to wear. Even though I was about to go on a date with someone I already knew and whom I had met nearly twenty years ago; I still wanted to make a good impression.

Walking towards Old Compton Street, I could feel myself getting anxious. And my ribs were still giving me a twinge of pain now and again. I stopped outside one of the pubs and saw two handsome looking specimens holding hands across a table, gazing lovingly into each other's eyes.

That could end up being me and Travis.

No, don't get your hopes up. The devil on my opposite shoulder replied.

ME: I need a slap.

*TULLENE: *sends slap emoji**

ME: I'm so nervous.

TULLENE: It's 7:07. You're late!

ME: I've waited almost twenty years. Ten more minutes is not going to make much difference.

TULLENE: True dat.

Turning the corner, I spotted the G-A-Y bar and then surveying the street, Travis caught my eye. My heart started racing. I could hear it beating loudly in my ears. I froze to the spot. My feet wanted to move but it was as though someone had superglued them to the pavement. I must have had an out of body experience because the next thing I remember is Travis speaking which snapped me out of my trance.

"I told you we'd naturally spot each other!"

"TRAVIS!"

"What you doing standing here?"

I couldn't give an answer to that. Nerves probably but I wasn't going to let him in on that secret.

"I got distracted by Tullene texting me."

"Tullene! How is she?"

"Listen, let's get a drink and then I can tell you all the news."

And then he hugged me and gave me a peck on the cheek. I did get a little breathless. And no, I hadn't suddenly developed asthma. Travis genuinely made my heart flutter. And he had done since I was a mere 17 year old.

We walked into G-A-Y bar and I suddenly felt like I'd aged twenty years. I know I don't look my age of forty years but I'm sure some of the people frequenting this drinking establishment were not even of a legal drinking age.

"Jesus. Is there a secondary school outing going on?" I joked to Travis.

"To think we were that age once."

"Oh don't. Over twenty years ago. And you were trying to rape me on Lizzie's bedroom floor."

Travis went the colour of a tomato. He broke the awkward silence.

"Glass of Savvy B?"

"Bottle!" I said incredulously. "Don't insult me!"

"Sorry. Didn't mean to offend." And we both roared with laughter. And I felt myself drawn to the dimple on his cheek when he laughed. It felt so natural together. Like we'd known each other for years. Which I know we had. But you catch my drift.

"And you can pay considering you've made me wait so long." I was half joking but also wanting to make a point in a light hearted manner.

And there it was again. Travis's impression of a tomato. I quite liked my ability to embarrass him. I found it endearing.

We sat down and indulged in the bottle of New Zealand plonk. My god, he can pack it away. I thought I was a lush but Travis can knock it back like he's in the navy. Why do we always assume that sailors are pissheads?

Before we knew it, the bottle had nothing but drips left in the bottom and I was up buying another. We felt quite squiffy by the time we had polished off the second.

I love that word, SQUIFFY. Sounds so much better than pissed or tipsy. SQUIFFY. An informal British slang saying meaning slightly drunk.

"I better get going soon", Travis informed me, looking at his watch. "My last train is in ten minutes."

We both felt a twang of sadness that the date had ended so soon. Travis had been very tactile with me all night, holding my hand, brushing my arm, stroking my leg. But no kiss had arrived. Until now.

We locked lips and it felt like the most passionate kiss I had experienced in a long time. It was like it was meant to be. Out of the corner of my eye, I saw some fireworks exploding over Big Ben. The colours were beautiful and seeing them at that exact moment in time made me feel so happy. It was like that kiss was in my destiny.

After what seemed like a lifetime, Travis pulled away from my lips and popped THE question.

"Do you want to come back to mine?"

But no, I didn't want to. Yes, I'd been a bit of a slag over the years and had had my fair share of one night stands but I didn't want that to be it for me and Travis. Call me old fashioned, but I wanted to wait until a later date to have sex. There was something more between us and I wanted to discover it.

Keep your audience wanting more. I think Shakespeare coined that phrase.

CHAPTER 13

A spray tan and a blow job (the next day. And a few days after that…)

"Well. You could knock me down with a feather." Those were the first words to leave Tullene's mouth when I told her I hadn't shagged Travis or gone home with him. "That's the shock of my life, that is." Those were the second words.

"I just want to wait until I see him again."

"Fair enough. Have you heard from him?"

"Yes, he WhatsApped me this morning."

TRAVIS: It was so lovely to see you. I had a fantastic time last night. It went way too quickly.

ME: Thank you for a lovely evening. I could have stayed with you much longer. It was over way too quickly. You're so handsome, adorable and funny. I hope to see you very soon.

TRAVIS: Everything you said about me is right back at you. I can't believe it had been that many years since I last saw you. It felt like only yesterday since I first met you. Let's get another date in the diary.

"That's all very positive!" Tullene's third words. "I take everything I said about him back because I had my doubts about him coming good."

"May God forgive you", I joked.

"Oh fuck off!"

"Nice Tullene."

ME: When you get a minute, send me over some dates you can do in the next week. And we can arrange to do something together. Have a lovely day on the railway, my little fat controller.

My pet name didn't really suit Travis as he's rather toned and as slim as a garden rake. But he's a train driver, so it was funny in my little mind.

It was nearly twenty four hours before he responded to my last text. But he's just busy on the railway, I told myself. I mean, he can't exactly check his phone whilst he's driving a train. Just as my eyes were starting to close that night, my WhatsApp tone pinged and gave me a right start.

TRAVIS: Mr Morgan!!! How have you been today? Hopefully you've had a better day than I fucking have! I've not stopped all bloody day. You calling me the fat controller does make me laugh. I'm livid. I've been covering for a colleague who is sick again. AND YES, I will definitely send over some dates.

ME: Oh my poor little fat controller having a tough day. I hope you have a better day tomorrow. If anyone gives you any grief, just send them to me. I'll give the cunts a slap round the chops!

And then he didn't reply. And he didn't send me any dates. Not that night anyway.

"I told you I had my doubts about him!" Tullene bellowed through the phone line.

Bemused, I chuckled to myself.

"You've changed your tune since yesterday morning."

I decided that I wasn't going to sit around worrying about it. He was obviously very busy. And after all, he did have a history of being absolutely rubbish at commitment, time lines and making plans. I needed to keep myself distracted and what better way than to go and help in my friend's salon. She had phoned me the night before because her receptionist had called in sick. And being the kind hearted soul that I am, I agreed to assist.

Sitting on reception, a beautiful man walked in. Perfect distraction material.

"Can you do a spray tan mate?" So butch. "I'm just on leave from the army and I need to get some colour on me to look good for my bird. She ain't seen me for months."

I went a little shy. Actually, that's like saying Hitler was a LITTLE nasty. I went full scale shyness. Crimson face, the works. He was butch, gobsmackingly gorgeous AND an army boy. It was just a shame that he wasn't in his uniform. And what a shame about his degrading language towards women but a flash of his perfect pearly whites and I'd momentarily forgiven the remark where he'd referred to his girlfriend as a flying species.

I checked the computer to see if my friend's salon could in fact accommodate this beautiful soldier for a spray tan.

"Erm. Well, someone could do it for you in an hour."

"Can't you do it now? You're just sat there."

I gulped. And my hands went a bit clammy. I was qualified and fully able to perform spray tans but I didn't know if I trusted myself not to get a boner.

"O...ok...okay." GREAT. I'd developed a stutter. "Come through."

Taking him to the tanning booth, I tried my hardest to remain professional. What an unfortunate choice of words, considering my fear of getting an erection. *You've seen plenty of naked men in your time.* I kept repeating to myself. And then Satan would appear on my opposite shoulder. *But none of them have looked like this.*

Handing him a disposable thong, he chucked it to the table on the side.

"I don't need to wear that. I don't want any tan lines."

I gulped an even deeper gulp. As he stripped his clothes off, I felt beads of sweat dripping from my botoxed forehead. All whilst manifesting thoughts of my dead grandma to stop my penis from reacting to what my eyes were about to witness.

As he removed his top, it was obvious he worked out MULTIPLE times a day and his abs looked like they'd never even heard the word carbohydrate, let alone eaten one. As his boxer shorts slid down his legs, I kept repeating my mantra.

GRANDMA MORGAN! GRANDMA MORGAN! DEAD GRANDMA MORGAN!

Fuck me, I had a canoe staring back at me. I'd never seen a cock like it. I could have gone kayaking down the Thames on his penis. Feeling soldier boy's eyes watching me, I averted my gaze from his girthy ginormous member.

I picked up the spray tan gun and started spraying him up and down with the St Tropez glow.

"And turn!"

Oh my days. What an arse. It looked like two hard boiled eggs in a clutch bag. So pert.

Getting him to turn to face me once more, I noticed he had a couple of white bits left on either side of his thighs where said canoe was blocking my ability to give him an even spritz on his upper legs.

"Erm." I could feel my face turning crimson. "Could you just move your…" I took a deep breath as I suddenly retrograded to my five year old self who couldn't muster themselves to say the word. "Erm, can you move your penis to the side so I can spray up your legs."

He shrugged. "You can do it. I don't care if you touch it."

Too nervous to actually make complete contact, I found myself doing an impression of swatting a fly and was lightly tapping his massive tool to move it to the side. Realising my technique wasn't getting the job done, he grabbed my hand and forcibly wrapped it around his manhood. At which point, I could feel something growing between my own thighs.

"Do you wanna suck it?" He posed the very forward question and that particular service was not included in the price, but I decided to oblige. And before you could say fake tan, I was on my knees with a canoe between my lips.

After going above and beyond with my customer service, I bid my army man a good day. I don't know why I'm talking like someone from a Victorian novel. I said goodbye and ran to the toilet to check my face for any evidence.

Grinning like a Cheshire cat and high fiving myself for sucking off such a fit guy, I stopped in my tracks as I caught a glimpse of the reflection staring back at me in the mirror.

My teeth had turned an interesting shade of orange. This is awkward.

CHAPTER 14

The Great British Shave Off (December 2018)

Two whole weeks and I'd still heard nothing from Travis. So much for him sending me some dates. Tullene was telling me to forget about him.

"Fuck him. If he can't be bothered to organise a second date, then screw him. You can do better."

Tullene changes her mind and opinions as often as the British weather. Buttplug, on the other hand, is a little more diplomatic when it comes to these matters.

"If you really think there's something between you, then YOU take control and YOU send him dates for him to pick from."

I chose the latter friend's advice.

ME: How are you Mr Travis? So, because waiting for you is like waiting for Jesus to return, here's some dates I can do over the next week or so. Sunday? Wednesday? Or Saturday afternoon? I hope one of those might work for you.

TRAVIS: Hello Mr Mark Morgan!!! I'm so sorry for my lack of contact. I'll be perfectly honest and say I've been drinking wine today and I'm defi-

nitely not sober right now. So I will reply properly tomorrow.

ME: Enjoy your un-sober Sunday darling!

I wanted to say, I bet tomorrow never comes but I thought I'd channel Buttplug's diplomacy, in favour of Tullene's bulldozer approach. Let's see if tomorrow happens…

Meanwhile, I decided I needed a distraction. I looked in the mirror and noticed my precious spiky hair. Well, what was left of it. It had always been my signature. My trademark. It's why I'd loved mini GHD straighteners so much. They had always straightened my hair into my outrageous sticky-up design. Followed by a generous lathering of hairspray to hold it in place. I think the ozone layer breathed a sigh of relief once I'd gone bald.

But my hair was now hanging on by a root. Pun intended. The fate of my hair follicles were decided as soon as Mummy Morgan chose to pro-create with Daddy Morgan. Unfortunately he was bald before he was forty. For which he blames marrying my mother but genetically, I knew I never had a chance of keeping my hair much past forty.

And in recent years, I'd seen my hair falling away quicker than a Katie Price, AKA Jordan song leaving the top 40. So that day, there and then, I decided it was time to take action.

I couldn't control the fate of Travis and how that would pan out but I could control the hair that was on top of my scalp. Well, what was left of it.

"Tullene. I'm gonna shave my hair off."

I heard a thud. I hoped she hadn't fainted.

"Tullene?"

"Sorry. I dropped my phone. It was the shock."

"The time has come. My hair is getting too thin on top and it's starting to look stupid."

"I will support you." She reassured me. She knew this was a big deal for me.

"Thank you. It means I will have to give up the fake tan too."

I heard another thud.

"Tullene?"

"Can you please stop. I can't take any more shocks today. Plus I can't afford to have my phone replaced."

I knew I couldn't go on with smearing on the fake tan once I was a baldy. I would look like a half-eaten Malteser.

Anybody who knows me well, knows how vain I am and how important my appearance is. This was a BIG deal.

But who knows? With my new butch look, I could attract a whole new type of man.

I wouldn't be a twink anymore. Although, let's face it, I'm forty now and been grasping onto the 'twink' label for far longer than I probably should have.

I grabbed the electrical shaver and raised it to my scalp. And as I saw my gorgeous spiky locks fall to the floor, instead of being melancholic, I smiled and decided to embrace my inevitable baldness.

CHAPTER 15

The Rugby Tackle (January 2019)

New Year, New Me. I felt re-born as a slaphead poofter. My new image was getting me attention from a completely different type of bloke.

Whilst walking to get a pint of milk one morning, I'd been wolf whistled at by a couple of butch builders. And whilst doing some reps on the leg press at the gym one day, I'd been chatted up by a rather dishy bodybuilder. Now I was a baldy, it seemed I had a whole new buffet to sample.

"To think I was dreading going bald." Tullene was on the phone for our daily conference call.

"It's because you've got a perfectly shaped head. You suit it."

"Oh, I know. I thank God for it. If my head was a dodgy shape and I didn't suit it, I would have taken out a loan and invested in a hair transplant."

"Did you ever hear from Travis?"

The fact we both have ADHD means our phone conversations regularly jump from one topic to another.

"Funny you should ask that. I got a text this morning", I paused for dramatic affect. "AFTER NEARLY A MONTH." And I raised my voice for, well, not dramatic affect but just to show I was generally pissed off with said man.

TRAVIS: Hello Mr Mark!!! I hope you are okay my darling. Please do not think I have been neglecting you. I have literally had the most horrendous time at work. I'm completely stressed out with my workload. PLEASE PLEASE PLEASE do not think this neglect is any reflection on how I feel about you. I genuinely cannot wait to meet up again. But I promise I want to plan a date ASAP.

"Ignore the bastard!" Tullene advised me in her capacity as best friend.

I felt I needed the more diplomatic opinion of Buttplug.

"I would ignore him and never reply again." No swearing but the same advice came from my other friend too.

"Oh I intend to. If you can't make the effort and show up in a timely manner, I'm not going to give you the time of day."

"He's had more chances than he deserved." Tullene and Buttplug echoed each other.

"Exactly! And now I'm moving on. Travis is not the love of my life as I'd thought all these years. If he was, he'd be here now with no effort or questions or confusion."

So I didn't reply to him. And instead, I opened Grindr.

STAN, 51. WELL BUILT. RUGBY PLAYER.

I mean, there was other information on his profile but I stopped reading after I saw he was a partaker in the sport involving tackling. Most people's bucket lists include visiting the Taj Mahal. Or bungee jumping. Or maybe a ride in a hot air balloon. Shagging a rugby player had always ranked particularly high on mine. So I quickly got my fingers typing to him.

ME: Would you like to tackle my balls?

I high fived myself in the mirror. I thought I was being clever. He obviously appreciated my humour.

STAN: You're fit mate. I love a bald man.

Another high five to myself. Thank god I'd got the razor out before Christmas. My new found baldness was serving me well.

STAN: Do you want to come over and I'll show you how I handle a ball?

ME: As long as you get me in a scrum.

STAN: Oh, I'll get my head down and gain possession of your ball. Don't you worry about that.

The joy of potentially dating a rugby player meant the possibilities for puns were endless. Well, I use the word dating. I hadn't even met him yet. And besides that, it was highly likely I was only going to be participating in one game on Stan's team.

Before you could say *TOUCH,* I was at Stan's flat and ready to be taken *ADVANTAGE* of.

Stan had obviously taken the trouble of ACTUALLY reading my Grindr profile as he had an ice cold glass of Savvy B waiting for me when I arrived. One point to him.

"It's from New Zealand", he informed me as he placed the glass in my hand.

Two points. I was impressed. A few sips later and our lips were in a scrum of their own. He was so beefy and I was so excited to be ticking off a bucket list item. Oh this rugger boy was lush.

As penetration got underway, Stan rolled on top of me and I heard a *CRACK!* I stopped thrusting my hips for a moment.

"MY RIBS!" I cried out. Stan was taken aback at my yelp.

"What's happened?"

"I think you've cracked one of me ribs. They've only just healed from when I broke them a few months ago."

With all the commotion, I hadn't registered my penis was actually still inside him.

"Do you wanna cum?" Nice. I'm glad he was so concerned about my rib predicament. But it did seem a little rude not to ejaculate, considering I was still inside him.

"I'll take one for the team!" I screamed.

But as orgasm was about to be reached, Stan started rolling about like a gymnast and I had to push him off.

"You're not the size to be rolling on top of people!" It was starting to hurt to breathe. I could tell that I'd definitely damaged my ribcage once again.

Lying in bed that night, dosed up on paracetamol and ibuprofen, I saw a message pop up on my screen.

STAN: Can I see you again?

ME: No. I'm sorry but I can't afford the ribs.

That time I became a bottom bitch (February 2019)

I was out of action for a few more weeks again after being rugby tackled to within an inch of my life. And my bloody ribs cracking once more. Luckily it had been Christmas and new year very recently, so my wine cellar was well stocked up from Christmas gifts. Well, I say wine cellar. It's actually a wine rack on top of my kitchen work top. But nevertheless, there was plenty of booze to be guzzled to take the edge off. Purely medicinal of course. For the pain.

There's no such thing as Dry January in my world. Talking of dry, I had been feeling rather dehydrated. And I'm not talking about lack of water. It had been nearly two months since I'd had any kind of connection with a man. And I was starting to feel the effect of repetitive strain injury in my wrist from pleasuring myself.

And as though by magic, a text popped up from an old flame. Well, I say a flame. I'd seen him once. In the back of a taxi. When he was driving me home from a birthday party.

Remember Ahmed? My uber driver? He definitely got five stars on his rating from me that night. I wasn't best pleased that he only gave me four stars on my customer profile!

"I sorry. I pressed four by mistake", he apologetically told me when I questioned him. I say questioned; it was more of an interrogation.

AHMED: You like sex?

I was tempted to reply with, *YES, I love it.* But I knew that in Ahmed's broken English that this wasn't actually a question about whether I enjoyed carnal pleasure. It was his way of asking if I'd like to see him for a bunk up.

ME: Yes please!

Now, for anybody who knows me sexually or just for anybody who knows about my preference within the bedroom, I am a top. I can count on the fingers of one hand how many times I have been on bottom duty.

It's always scared me. The thought of anything or anyone entering my back passage. For those of you who may have taken deliveries in their back door will know what I mean. I personally feel like I'm going to shit myself. And then all over the delivery driver to boot. Pardon the pun.

It also doesn't feel like the most pleasurable experience. But then again, that's just me. I know some people who adore it and say it's the best thing since sliced bread. After all, a male's G spot is the prostate. Which, for those of you with rubbish anatomical knowledge, is located just inside the rectum. The posh name for your bottom.

Maybe I don't have a G spot which is why I find no joy in accepting gifts up the rectum.

AHMED: You bottom today?

I didn't need a degree in broken English to work that one out. I gulped. A rather big gulp. Probably too big of a gulp actually as I found myself with a bit of indigestion after that.

ME: I will try. But I'm not promising.

Before you could say hole in one, Ahmed was in my flat with his trousers down and his Egyptian sausage flapping about in my face.

My eyes widened. And I could feel my bottom hole constricting like a python. Coming face to face with Ahmed's penis in broad daylight gave me a shock. I hadn't realised quite how well-endowed he was. After all, I'd only seen it when I was in a drunken state in the back of a dark taxi.

"You take it?"

I felt my back door narrow further.

"If you can get it in, you're welcome to try."

As I saw it start its journey towards my bottom, I could feel my pulse beating in my hole. As a distraction, I dropped to my knees and wrapped my mouth around his meat. I knew I would have no trouble taking it in that compartment of my body. I've always been very competent when it comes to accommodating a penis in that hole.

But my blow job didn't prove to divert his attention for too long. He obviously had his mind set on that pork sausage finding a home in my tight, almost virgin butt.

Realising my fate, I flooded myself downstairs with KY Jelly. You could have sailed the Titanic down there the amount I slapped on. I decided all I could do now was damage limitation. The things we do to please our lovers.

I felt his ship sail away down my ocean and I suddenly had a suspicion that I might have some idea how the captain felt as he hit that iceberg on that fateful night back in 1912.

"SHIT!" I screamed.

What an unfortunate choice of word considering exactly where Ahmed had his cock right then in that moment.

I remember some advice Billy had once given me on one of my gay walks...

"It's the first 30 seconds that are the worst. Breathe through them and then you might start to enjoy it!"

Remember Billy? I'd quite fancied him when he attended the first ever gay walk I led. But I'd not seen him again since. I wonder what ever happened to him... *SPOILER ALERT:* You will find out very soon as I saw him again in the summer of 2019.

Taking deep breaths as though I were in labour, I counted to 30 seconds, praying that Billy's words of wisdom were in fact correct. I'm no mathematical genius but I was sure I'd gotten to 45 seconds and still I felt like I was being fingered by an elephant.

I heard Ahmed orgasm and was sure I felt something wet inside me. Unless that was KY Jelly still slipping and slopping about. Never did I ever think that I would be so relieved to have a man cum so quickly.

"GET IT OUT!" I bellowed. And he did as he was told. And then he also left rather abruptly.

Laying in bed the next morning, Tullene's name popped up on my phone screen.

"Morning!" She was jollier than normal. "How's your arsehole?" And cruder than her usual self.

"I'm never bottoming again. I managed to get it in my mouth alright. But when it came to the anus..."

"Perhaps you should try it with a man who is less well endowed."

She was probably right of course. Not that I would ever admit that to her as she can be rather smug as it is.

CHAPTER 16

Billy (July 2019)

Now cast your minds back to when I led my first ever gay walk back in 2016. There was a rather handsome chap by the name of Billy who caught my eye. And he flirted with me outrageously and of course, I requited and reciprocated his efforts. But then he never appeared on another walk again. Until the summer of 2019 during a holiday to the Cotswolds.

Every summer my gay walking group hold a, what they call, AOG. To educate you, that stands for Annual Outdoor Gathering. I grant you; it does sound like a posh version of 'dogging' but I assure you it's not.

"I'm off to the Cotswolds!" I screamed down the line to Buttplug.

Tullene must have been on holiday this particular morning so Buttplug had taken over the duties of a morning conference call.

"Oh yes. It's your dogging holiday."

I pursed my lips. For all the good said action did as I was on a voice call with her so she wouldn't have seen my reaction anyway.

"You should definitely get laid this weekend", she continued, "on holiday for four days with all those other gay men."

"I should be so lucky. I think you've forgotten I bring the median age range down to about FIFTY!"

It was true. As much as I loved all my fellow gay walkers, you were lucky to find one who was below 70. They're all members of God's waiting room, as my Dad likes to say.

My father is full of the dry, witty humour. I remember one day my mum called me up to complain about him. She'd phoned to moan about my father's "abnormal behaviour" as she refers to it.

"Your dad keeps opening up the curtains when we wake up in the morning."

"That's not too abnormal mum."

"But it's what he says as he opens them."

"Here we go…"

"Mark, he pulls them open, looks up to the sky, takes a deep breath and turns to me to say, I wonder how many more mornings we have left!"

Anyway, I've digressed from my conference call with Buttplug, actually known as Sarah. She was right though; it would have been lovely to get a bit of how's your father on my mini break with the gays. I hadn't had sex since February after my encounter with Ahmed.

"I think this is the longest I've ever gone. My desert is dry." I informed her.

"I think you've got PTSD, that's post traumatic stress disorder."

"Thank you for clarifying what PTSD is, just in case I didn't know," I barked sarcastically but it fell on deaf ears. "Why have I ended up with two best friends who like to psychoanalyse me?" Buttplug continued her impression of a psychiatrist.

"Just shut up and listen. Ahmed has put you off sex because you decided to bottom for him and then couldn't sit down without an inflatable rubber ring for a week."

It sounded like a fabricated tale but alas, it was all true. I hadn't been able to sit down properly after that fateful incident.

"And don't forget the thrush in my throat a week after sucking him off!" I reminded her.

Yes, sadly that part was no lie either. I remember the phone call I had made to Tullene a week after bottom-gate to inform her I was having trouble swallowing.

"You don't normally have a problem with that," she responded.

I chose to ignore her attempt at a joke.

"It's really sore too and I'm talking about my throat."

"Get to the doctors!"

I did as I was told and marched myself down to the family doctor, Dr Kullar. Oh, he's a lovely man, been our doctor since I was a teenage boy so to be sat opposite him, knowing I may have an STI from giving a blow job mortified me. I couldn't bring myself to tell him the full story so I just feigned a sore throat.

"Maybe I've got tonsillitis doctor."

"Open wide then!" Doctor Kullar instructed as he came towards me with his tongue depressor.

Too soon, I thought. I was triggered by being told to open wide after Ahmed's invasion of my fort.

For those of you who are wondering what a tongue depressor is; it's one of those light coloured stick things the doctor rams down your gob when they want to investigate your tonsils. Or for those who prefer the proper medical definition…

A simple class I medical device. It is intended for use during the course of a medical examination to depress the tongue in order to allow the clinician an easier examination of the mouth and throat.

"Come on!"

I still hadn't opened wide for the doc.

He came lunging at me with his depressor, got it half way in my mouth and I gagged. I pushed his tool away abruptly. Doctor Kullar looked shocked.

"You can't put that in my mouth. I'll be sick all over you."

I know you will all be aghast at this but I don't have the best gag reflex. That is contrary to popular belief, especially knowing the amount of male genitalia that have graced my lips over the years.

"I need to put this in your mouth otherwise I can't examine you."

The pun hadn't escaped me but I was in no mood at that particular moment to appreciate it.

"I don't know why I gag on your stick thingy doctor. I can deep throat a cock but you come near me with that and…"

I could see the look of shock that spread across my physician's face so I decided it was best to not finish that sentence. I wanted the ground to swallow me up. I couldn't seem to stop the words from leaving my mouth.

Doctor Kullar cleared his throat. "Indeed."

Very diplomatic response.

I eventually arrived in the Cotswolds and I pulled up in the fire service college car park.

No, I hadn't taken the wrong turning. You may or may not know this but there is a college in the Cotswolds which provides training for emergency services. And they also provide accommodation for groups holidaying. Well, if I couldn't lay a gay walker, the next best thing could be a fireman. Now, the possibilities for puns there are endless but I won't be so basic as to mention their hoses just yet. Oops, too late!

As I grabbed my room key from reception, I climbed the stairs to my floor. I was on the third floor and the lift was out of order. I hoped some of the older gentlemen weren't on that floor with the lift out of service. If I was out of breath at the age of 40, they'd be dead by the time they got to their room.

As I scanned my keycard on room 307, I heard a voice boom from behind me. I didn't recognise it.

"Led any decent walks lately? Discovered any new breeds of cow or sheep?"

And then it dawned on me. I remembered that joke he played on me making up the random breed of cow sheep. I did a quick turnabout on my heels and was greeted by none other than BILLY.

Thank god I'd had my botox topped up and my eyebrows touched up. I smiled and he smiled straight back. He was even more gorgeous than I'd remembered.

"Billy!" I gasped. Not because I was shocked to see him but because I'd just climbed all those stairs and I'm not the fittest and was trying to catch my breath.

"You remember my name?" He sounded impressed.

"How could I forget you?"

His eyes dazzled like diamonds and he grinned like a giraffe. He was obviously touched that I'd remembered him after three years.

"Would you like to go grab a glass of wine together?" He wasn't backward in coming forward.

"Now?"

"No. Next week." I like a man who can match me in sarcasm.

How could I refuse?

"Let me dump my suitcase and then I want a large Savvy B!"

Billy and the fire alarm (A few minutes later- and then the next day and maybe the day after that)

I remember staring at myself in the mirror for about five minutes after closing my accommodation door. I could feel it in the pit of my gut that I had a connection with Billy. I had butterflies that he'd asked me to go for a glass of plonk.

But then my inner saboteur kicked in. I remembered having similar thoughts when it came to Travis. And look how that turned out.

ME: I can't do it.

TULLENE: Do you need me to drive to the Cotswolds and slap your face?

You can always rely on Tullene for some plain-spoken advice. But I suppose that's what best friends are for. I've given her my fair share of frank opinions over the years.

ME: But I'm scared. I don't want to get involved with another man if it's going to end up not going anywhere.

TULLENE: Not every man is going to do what Travis did. Do you want to die alone?

ME: NO.

TULLENE: Then you mustn't give up. Even when the chips are down, you always pick yourself up, brush yourself down and carry on.

ME: Exactly! I'm Mark Morgan!

Tullene had managed to give me the slap I needed without any physical violence involved. Just some candid text conversation.

I had got to the point where all I wanted from men was sex. This way, I told myself, you couldn't get hurt. You'd get a bit of the other and then ask them to leave.

"But that's no way to find a connection with a man. Not on a deeper level", Buttplug had often warned me when I preached my mantra that men are only for sex. You couldn't have two best friends more different. But that's what I need in my life. One who gives me the no-nonsense approach. And one who is a little more sensitive. Yin and yang. I think everyone should have a Tullene and Buttplug in their lives.

I powdered my nose with my anti-shine papers to make sure I was looking the best I could for Billy. Has anyone tried those anti-shine papers? If you haven't, then you really should. They're perfect for giving you a matte finish and an even complexion when you want to look your best.

I meandered into the bar at the fire service college. I know right, I too was shocked to find a bar here, albeit the size of a garden shed. But I guess all those big butch firefighters need a drink after saving lives all day. And yes, I know there's also female fire people but I don't find that particular species attractive. Just the male ones with their hoses…

"MARK!" Billy calling out my name interrupted what was about to become pornographic thoughts.

I gave him a little wave and approached his table. Only one glass of wine in front of him. Not a good start. Where was mine?

"Glad to see you got me a drink."

"You've got legs and arms, haven't you?", came his retort.

I playfully gestured two fingers in his face and headed up to the two metre bar. I felt a hand slap my bottom. That's a bit forward, I thought. But it wasn't Billy.

"You old poofter!" I knew that wasn't Billy's voice. I recognised that dulcet tone. I span on my heels to be greeted with Robert. Remember Robert? My gay best friend who was first drawn to my eyebrows and we've been mates ever since.

"What you doing?"

I wanted to tell him I was about to have a drink with a man I really fancied and who was potentially husband material but Robert has the discretion of a town crier so I downplayed it. I turned to point at Billy.

"Remember Billy? He came on one of the walks I led. We're just getting a drink."

"Oh hello love! Your face rings a bell but my memory ain't what it once was!"

Talking of friends you should have, Robert is also one of them. Just hearing him speak always cheers me up, even when I don't think I need cheering.

"So is this a date?" Robert winked at me deliberately conspicuously. And he wanted to ensure Billy witnessed said wink.

I gave him my best death glare but Robert being Robert took absolutely no notice. As Billy had quite obviously noticed the exchange between us, I decided to embrace it rather than pretending it didn't exist.

"You do know Billy can see and hear everything?" Robert was unperturbed.

I caught a smile from Billy.

"Well boys. I'll leave you to it. And don't do anything I wouldn't do!" Robert screamed at both of us, planting a big kiss on my cheek.

"It's going to be a very boring night then!" Billy had the ability to match Robert in wit, sarcasm and playfulness.

I could tell Robert approved. Anybody who could match him in outrageousness was granted a seal of approval.

Finally getting my hands on a large Savvy B, I took a huge glug and raised my glass to Billy.

"Cheers!"

We sat in the bar for the rest of the night, taking it in turns to replenish one another with a wet beverage. I lost count of how many I knocked back that night. I'd had more than I cared to remember. Once Billy had two heads, I decided it was time for me to get to my bed.

Not only could he match me in sarcasm and acerbic wit but he also managed to put away as much Savvy B as me. I found this particularly impressive as I can drink most men under the table. I know that's not a party trick one should really brag about as it borders on alcoholic behaviour. I stood up and stumbled a little but saved myself. Winning.

"I think I should probably join you."

I misunderstood Billy's meaning.

"Oh, I'm in no fit state for any of that how's your father. I probably won't even be able to get it up."

Awkward silence, followed by embarrassed laughter as I realised he meant he should take himself to bed too. Not actually join me in mine.

We staggered back to our rooms. And it really was a stagger as the lifts were still broken. I could tell I was going to have bruised shins in the morning the amount of stairs I tripped up.

Billy walked me all the way back to my door. And I praised the Lord he did as I found myself unable to navigate using the access key to gain entry to my room.

"Thank you. You're so nice and you make me laugh." Billy pecked me on the cheek. I went in for one on the lips but he pushed me off.

AWKWARD.

"Not yet. I like you. Goodnight Mark."

I inhaled deeply. My stomach felt as though it were on a spin cycle. I watched Billy disappear into his room and then I managed to fiddle about to get inside my own.

Collapsing fully clothed on the bed, I managed to close one eye to enable me to focus on my phone screen so I could text. I couldn't remember who I was trying to type to but no doubt Tullene or Buttplug.

ME: In love. Got on so well. Thing might I narry this men. Didn't evrn kiss. Must br true love.

And then I face planted the pillow. Even an earthquake wouldn't have woken me up that night. And it wasn't until the very next morning that I realised just how accurate that statement was.

Struggling to focus as my eyes opened, my lashes were stuck together from mascara. Yes from time to time, I slap some on to make my eyes even more pretty. My mouth felt like the bottom of a birdcage. My head had several dwarves in it, tapping away with hammers. I managed to grasp hold of my phone and saw a text.

It was from Billy; *when did I even get his number? I couldn't remember.*

BILLY: Like to NARRY me, would you? I need to see your performance in the sack first.

FUCKING. SHIT. HOLY. SHIT. I don't know what I was more mortified about. My appalling spelling in the message or the fact my words meant for one of my best friends had landed in Billy's inbox.

I thought it best to ignore Billy's reply for the moment. I was in no fit state to deal with that at that minute. I needed CARBS. A carb fuelled breakfast inside me before I made any life choices.

Tripping over my feet on the way to the breakfast room, I imagined everybody was staring at me. And no, I hadn't dropped a pill before breakfast. It was just drunk hangover paranoia kicking in.

"Where were you last night you old queen?" Robert's shrill certainly slapped me out of my Savvy B induced coma.

"Not so loud", I begged.

"Got a hangover, have we?" He continued in his piercing tone. "Don't look now but here comes Billy."

"Oh no, Robert. Hide me! He can't see me in this state!" Wrong person to ask for discreet help.

"Coo-ey!" Robert added a wave, just to ensure Billy didn't miss us.

"Morning Mark! Robert." Billy was just as handsome with a hangover. I didn't think I was, so I tried to hide my face but to no avail.

"You must have been dead to the world after I walked you home last night."

"Oh I was. Passed out."

"We noticed", Robert chipped in, "you didn't even wake up to the fire alarm going off at 2am this morning."

"Fire alarm?" I was bemused. I hadn't heard a thing.

"Yes", Billy continued, "went off and we all had to gather outside in our pants and dressing gowns."

And then it dawned on me. Everybody had left me to burn to death.

"Oh. Well I'm glad you all knocked on my door to check I was alive."

Billy informed me that when they realised it was just a technical fault, they'd decided it wasn't worth waking me up. I had to tell Tullene.

ME: I was so pissed I slept through a fire alarm. Nobody even checked I was alive.

TULLENE: You'll get over it.

And I knew I would but I was more gutted that I'd missed seeing Billy in his pants.

CHAPTER 17

Billy's revelation (The next day)

It was the last day of the AOG and I had managed to recover from that god awful hangover. I swear they get worse with age. When I was a mere whippersnapper of a twenty something gay boy, I could knock back ten pints and some vodka and still get up for work at 7am.

Yes, I know what you're thinking since I mentioned pints and vodka. I did used to have less refined tastes in alcoholic beverages when I was younger. Actually, it wasn't so much of a lack of refined tastes, it was more that I just didn't have the budget for said tastes. I wasn't yet able to afford the luxury of a sauvignon blanc from the Marlborough region in New Zealand.

What I was struggling to forgive was being left to perish in a fire. I at least thought Billy would have been concerned for my safety. I strolled into the breakfast room and noticed Billy sitting alone. I'll invite myself to join him, I decided.

He caught a glimpse of me before I'd had a chance to take a seat, uninvited, and his teeth glistened at me so I knew I was welcome at his table.

"Any fire alarm you want to tell me about that I might have slept through last night?" I joked as I gestured to the empty chair to indicate my intention of wanting to sit in it and to ask for any objections. He didn't have any. So I sat my bottom down at the table.

"No, no. You were safe last night."

"Not like the night before when I was left to be barbequed in my bed." I was really dragging out my feigned hurt.

"Don't be so dramatic, you little drama queen." I like a man who can put me in my place. And shut me up. And it looked like Billy could manage to do both. There's not many men that have been successful in rendering me speechless.

"Which walk you going on today?" Billy enquired.

"The one up that big hill." Geography has never been my strongest subject.

"You mean Bourton-on-the-hill?"

"If that's what it's called!"

"I'm going on that one too." Billy beamed.

"What a co-incidence. We get to spend a whole day together. Aren't you lucky?"

Billy feigned a look of horror.

"I think I'll just go and sign up for a different walk." We laughed. I feigned an insulted look. His sense of humour was on par with mine. Mischievous, sarcastic and I liked his witty comebacks.

As we walked up Bourton-on-the-hill, I could feel myself getting breathless. I was still smoking back then so my lungs didn't always work at full capacity. But as I was trying to remain alluring and fit to my walking companion, I pretended I could breathe perfectly fine. Smiling through gritted teeth to try and hide the fact I might have an asthma attack any second. And I don't even suffer from asthma.

I could feel my heart flutter as I looked at Billy and him at me. My hopes this walk would resemble a scene out of The Sound of Music and we would dance around, hand in hand on the hilltops, were dashed by my twenty a day fag habit. And the fact it had just started pissing down with rain didn't help matters either.

We got back to the rooms and looking like drowned rats escaping from a sinking ship, Billy escorted me to my door.

"You better get out those wet clothes", he instructed me.

"Are you gonna help me?" Those words just happened. As soon as they left my lips, I regretted them but my worries were unfounded.

Billy held my face in his hands and looked at me like no other man had ever looked at me before. Butterflies were doing a little dance in my stomach. Actually, it felt more like they were having a rave. As he kissed me on the lips, I could see an explosion of beautifully coloured fireworks over the mountaintops in the distance. Yes, I have a vivid imagination.

"I'm going to marry this man." Don't worry, I said that in my head and not out loud. Even I thought it was a bit soon to be making declarations of that sort.

I managed to scramble about and open my door with the key card. Still locked in a passionate embrace, we fell through the door and I kicked it shut with my foot as he lifted me up, a la Dirty Dancing style.

"I'm going to make love to you." My heart did a jig. No man had ever worded acts of sexual intercourse in that manner before. It had always been *I'm going to fuck you* or *let's shag!*

Laying in bed after the most passionate encounter of my life, Billy held me tight and I rested my head on his chest. He had beautiful nipples. Not too big like burger baps but not too small like smarties either. Just the perfect shape and size. Yes, you know I have a nipple fetish.

"I want to see you again. And again. And again." I just blurted it out. Before I would have held my cards a little closer to my pectoralis muscles for fear of being hurt.

"And I want to see you again." I had to ask for confirmation and clarification in case my hearing was playing up.

"You do?"

"But..." Oh holy fuck. Here we go.

"This moment has been so perfect. Why do I feel like this BUT is going to ruin it?"

"I'm moving to New Zealand for two years on a work secondment." I didn't need to respond. I was floored. Billy could see that his announcement had pulled the rug right from under my feet. Well, technically from under my back as I was laying down at the time of said announcement.

"That's a bit far for a long distance relationship", was all I could offer as a response.

And then I didn't see Billy again. Not for two years anyway.

You like my pussy baby? (August 2019)

TULLENE: Has his flight taken off yet?

ME: Yes. I'm tracking it on the airport app thingy.

TULLENE: Stalker.

ME: Hey. The man who I think is the one I'm going to marry is flying off into the sunset. Without me.

TULLENE: Well, you've now got two years to kill.

Tullene was right of course. Billy and I had come to an agreement that if we were both still single in two years' time when he got back to England, then we'd pick up where we left off.

But regardless of our arrangement, it still didn't stop me feeling broken hearted. I needed a distraction. GRINDR.

TARIN: You top?

ME: Yes.

TARIN SHARES LOCATION

ME: See you in fifteen.

Grindr never ceases to amaze me. The ease at which you can get an itch scratched. And probably catch a disease that causes itching into the bargain.

Tarin gave me about as much conversation in the flesh as he did via texting. Very little. And I say conversation, it was more of a grunt. But let's be frank, I wasn't going round for an in depth chat about life. He opened the door in a dressing gown, shut the door behind me, lifted his gown up and bent over. And who says romance is dead?

As penetration was underway, I'd come to the conclusion that Tarin might be mute. He let out a few groans of pleasure but that was it. Until out of nowhere…

"You like my pussy baby?"

I stopped mid-thrust as his outburst momentarily derailed my motion. And I had to do a quick check to ensure I was actually up the bum.

"You like fucking my pussy baby?" It was obviously his thing. His quirk. His fetish.

I continued penetration. If you can't beat them, join them, I decided.

"Oh yes! I love your pussy!" I exhaled as I came.

My Norwegian motorcyclist (September 2019)

After Billy flew off to New Zealand, I had a bit of a mid-life crisis. Well, I hope it wasn't actually MID-life because that means I'm going to die at eighty two. And I've always said to Tullene that I intend to live to a hundred!

I know some people who say they don't want to go on past eighty. I think they're mad. Obviously if I'm shitting myself and I need assistance to wipe my arse, then I'll reconsider my eagerness to reach the ripe old age of one hundred. But if I've got all my faculties and my body is in good working order, I want my telegram from the Queen. Although it's now KING (as of 2022-SPOILER alert LOL). And I also think you no longer receive a telegram as we're not in the 1950's. Probably a posh letter. But you catch my drift.

Anyway, said mid-life crisis encouraged me to take a trip to Norway. ON MY OWN.

"On your own?" Buttplug questioned.

"It's something I feel like I need to do."

"You're braver than me."

I know solo holidays are not for everybody. But I've always been perfectly comfortable in my own company. I've been to the theatre on my own. Eaten in a restaurant alone. It doesn't bother me.

"Can you drive me to the airport Butt?"

"When is it?"

"Tomorrow afternoon."

"As long as you help me move a bed first. I need to lift it out of my house, get it in my car and then drive it to my brothers."

Buttplug drives a hard bargain.

Lifting the bed from her front door to the boot of her car proved challenging for us and resembled a scene from the Chuckle Brothers.

Anyone younger than 40 will probably not have a clue who they are.

"TO ME."

"TO YOU."

As we began sliding the frame into the back of her Toyota, even a young child could have worked out that it was going to be a tight fit. One end of the frame was precariously sitting about an inch from the windscreen. Whilst the other end was resting a few centimetres from where the boot lid needed to shut.

Buttplug was on duty at the windscreen. There was no way I wanted to be responsible for the glass so I took the sensible option and stayed in charge of the rear end. No jokes please.

"Right. Hold your end tight whilst I close the boot." Still no jokes please.

My hand came down a bit hard on the handle and I slammed the boot lid down with a little more force than I had intended.

SMASH! The frame jolted against the windscreen and I saw it shatter into a million pieces. And no, I didn't count them but that's just how many fragments of glass it looked like. We didn't talk. For five whole minutes. I think it was the shock. We stood in complete silence, just gawping at the catastrophe that had just taken place in front of our eyes.

The first sound that left both of us was uncontrollable laughter. We couldn't stop for five whole minutes. It must have been the shock too.

And then after we'd finally come to and snapped out of our induced state of shock, I panicked about the time and if I would make it for my flight.

"Are you still going to be able to take me to the airport?"

Very selfish. It must have been the shock causing me to act in such a manner. Well, that's what I'm blaming anyway.

In spite of windscreen-gate, I still managed to make it to my terminal in time. There was no way I was missing that flight. I felt the trip to Norway was a rediscovering of myself. A chance to re-charge, re-set and wash away (metaphorically), some of the hurt of Billy moving to New Zealand.

And if I didn't catch a glimpse of the Northern lights, I wasn't going to be happy.

Sitting down for dinner in a beautiful little hotel, I was scouring the tour guides for the best places to view the Northern lights.

"I can help you see the Northern lights for free", I heard a Nordic accent boom across my dinner table.

Taken aback, I looked up and standing in front of me was a handsome blonde man, eyes fixated on me.

"I'm Arild."

"I'm Mark."

"You want me to take you to see those lights? Don't pay an expensive tour guide."

"What's the catch?"

"Don't be so cynical." He insisted.

As the main aim of me heading to Norway had been to catch a glimpse of the famous lights, I decided I didn't have anything to lose. Unless he was a psychopathic axe murderer of course but he seemed okay to me. Not that I have the best track record when it comes to judgement of men's characters and behaviours.

I stood up, excited to see the spectacle much sooner than I'd anticipated. And Arild actually pulled my chair out for me as I got up from the table and held my jacket up for me to slip my arms through. And who says chivalry is dead?

"You will need your jacket. It's very cold outside."

Heading out, we stopped at a motorbike. Perhaps he liked to admire such modes of transport. But as Arild opened the back box, my eyes widened as I realised it belonged to him. Unless he was about to commit an act of theft, to which I was soon to become an accessory.

"We're going on this?" I gave a nervous smile.

"Yes, yes. It will be… What's the word?"

Fucking death wish, I wanted to say but I refrained.

"…Liberating." He found the word.

Passing me a helmet, all I could think of was how grateful I was to now be bald. Because there was no way I would have put that on my head in the old days when I was still in possession of my perfectly coiffured spiky black hair.

"I hope it fits you", he began as I went to place said helmet on my bonce, "because you have very round, very large head…"

I was rendered speechless.

"…Like a football."

I managed to purse my lips and pushed the piece of motorbike safety apparatus down onto my *MASSIVE* head. I prayed it would fit as Arild obviously had his doubts. Now I know how on edge Cinderella must have felt as Prince Charming was shoving her foot into a random slipper.

I couldn't help doing a little celebratory jig as it slipped onto my football head with ease. Arild surveyed the scene, looking at me in the helmet. Finally, he gave his opinion.

"You look like you have downs syndrome."

I didn't get to see the Northern lights that night. Not because they weren't bright enough. But because I ripped the helmet off my head, threw it at Arild and told him to "Piss off!". I don't care if you tell me I have a head the size of America. But don't use an intellectual disability as an insult. That's a step too far in my book.

CHAPTER 18

That time I slept with a drag queen. In full drag. (Them, not me) October 2019

With my love for RuPaul's drag race, it had always been on my bucket list to shag a drag queen. And to perform the act whilst they were in FULL DRAG. I had always wondered if it would actually turn me on, especially as I like men. Who look like men. But there was only one way to find out.

I think the fantasy came from knowing that even though they are dressed to look like a woman, there was still a penis to be discovered underneath their frock. And a hole to be penetrated.

After the Northern lights debacle, and no, I never did get to see them. And no, I never saw that bastard again either. I can't even bring myself to say his name. I needed some drag in my life. So I *dragged*, yes, I am unashamed by my pun, Tullene and Buttplug to see a local drag show.

"Now don't sit there and get a boner", Tullene blurted out as we took our seats in the front row. Yes, front row. I wanted a good view.

The show began and I could feel a bead of sweat on my brow when Jemima Puddledick graced the stage in front of my eyes. I was in love.

I caught Jemima looking at me from the corner of her eye from time to time. Tullene must have noticed it too because she gave my arm a nudge.

"Your dreams could come true tonight if you play your cards right", Tullene whispered. But her whispering hadn't gone unnoticed. Jemima had spotted it and she stopped the show, looking directly at us. The auditorium was eerily silent and I heard Tullene gulp.

"Am I boring you both?" My drag wet dream boomed down her microphone.

We both shook our heads like naughty schoolchildren. But Jemima had made her decision. She was ready to name and shame us. And sprinkle us with embarrassment. Her long legs daintily came down the stage stairs towards us. Not just her legs obviously, the rest of her body followed too.

She plonked herself down on my lap. I prayed that she wouldn't feel anything pop up.

"So what's your name darling?" She purred seductively down the microphone, looking straight in my direction.

I went to hold her microphone to answer her question but she wrapped her hands tighter around it so I couldn't grab it.

"I'll tell you when you can hold it!" She screamed. "Just tell me your name."

"I'm Mark."

"So Mark darling. What's your favourite part of the show so far?"

"You." I wasn't shy in coming forward. Jemima was impressed.

"Good answer. I can tell we're going to get along swimmingly. And by swimmingly, I mean, I'll be wet."

The audience roared with laughter. I was more concerned with ensuring I didn't get an erection as I fancied Jemima even more close up.

"Would you like some more?", was her next question. I mean, she was actually talking about more of her drag show but little did Jemima know that I actually wanted to see more of her. And by more of her, I meant everything that was underneath her outfit.

She grabbed my hand and dragged me up onto the stage, declaring we were going to re-enact a scene from Oliver Twist.

"Give the lovely Mark a round of applause", she demanded as she got me onto the stage, "Everybody say hello to Mark!"

The whole theatre screamed my name.

"Now you say hello to them Mark."

"Alright everyone!" I beamed.

"We really are in a rougher part of London, aren't we?" Jemima sarcastically declared.

Now, Jemima next instructed me that I was to do my best impression of Oliver asking for some more food. Although this was a drag show so I assumed it was an innuendo for something else.

"Please sir, can I have some more?" I said in the sexiest voice I could muster. I deserved an Oscar for that performance. The audience were in hysterics. They were lapping it up.

"That was good, weren't it?" I asked them.

As they roared, YES!, Jemima snatched her microphone back.

"It wasn't quite Olivia Coleman but we have to work with what we've got."

And she gave me a once over, looked me right up and down. I could tell she wanted me as much as I wanted her.

"Now, we have to try it even sexier than that", Jemima teased as I was desperately ensuring my penis didn't go into erect mode in front of a live audience.

"Now, to achieve said sexiness", Jemima continued, "we have to try it with you in a certain position." My eyes widened. The audience going wild. "Now bend over!"

So, as I've always been one for discipline and for following the rules, I did as I was told and went down on all fours. Jemima came down behind me and I could feel her crotch resting on my coccyx. I came over all unnecessary.

"Now tell me you want some more!" She dictated. The audience were finding it highly entertaining. I was finding it rather arousing.

Making sure her microphone didn't pick up her next words, Jemima whispered in my ear.

"You better come to my dressing room after the show. Just wait in your seat and I'll get someone to show you in."

Well, that did it for me. I gave the best performance of my life. "Oh yes!," I screamed, "Go on. Give it to me, Gimme more!"

And little did the audience know that that night, life really did imitate art.

Suck for Daddy (November 2019)

I remember Jonathan. He was a schoolteacher with a fetish for baby/daddy role play. And he was one of the hairiest men that has ever graced my bedroom. I remember finding stray black chest hairs for weeks after his visit. Well, looking back, I'm not completely certain they were chest hairs.

There was only one problem with Jonathan. We were both tops. And what do two tops do when they end up together? Well, the first thing is normally a discussion.

"Will you bottom just for tonight?"

"HELL no!" I categorically bellowed. Jonathan gave a similar response when posed with the same question.

So as not to ruin the sexual vibe, I thought it was only polite I give him a blow job, being as though it was me who had invited him over. Mummy Morgan has always taught me to be very welcoming towards guests. I mean, I'm sure she probably means by offering them a cup of tea but as I don't drink tea, some oral sex had to suffice.

Before you could say one lump or two, Jonathan had dragged me up from my knees and insisted I start sucking on another part of his anatomy. His pec. Which was rather large. If I were a mean girl, I'd be tempted to call them moobs. Complete with burger nipples.

Before you could say milk with that?, he then had me cradled in his arms, a la baby style. Minus the nappy.

"Suck for Daddy!" He instructed me. "Does baby want some milk?" He asked.

To be polite and hospitable, I started "drinking milk" from Jonathan's moob. As I heard the noises leaving my mouth, I became rather impressed with myself. I didn't know I had such a talent when it came to creating sound effects. I could get a job on the radio. My newborn baby drinking milk from a boob was the first one I would add to my C.V.

CHAPTER 19

That time I had tequila and ended up face down in a gutter with a Mexican (January 2020)

Everybody has that one alcoholic beverage that they can't go near. The one they had such a bad experience with that it's put them off for life. Mine is tequila. And you shall soon find out why. I have vowed never to let the spirit ever grace my lips again.

"Let's go to Mexico!" Tullene declared during one of our morning conference calls.

I wasn't sure about holidaying with her so soon after Marbella. I was still waking up with night sweats, having nightmares about how she nearly drowned me in the pool.

"Oh go on!" She pleaded. "I promise not to go in the deep end of the swimming pool."

Before I could shout, TEQUILA, we appeared to be on an aeroplane heading towards Cancun for an all-inclusive trip to Mexico. It was a welcome break, if I'm honest, that I hadn't realised I'd needed.

"Two men Tullene. Two men in the last year that I thought were my soulmates and they've both gone tits up." I was feeling sorry for myself as I knocked back a piña colada from the hotel's cocktail menu.

"Don't get fucking melancholic," my holiday companion warned me. She'd already had two cocktails and I could tell by the tone of her voice she was on her way to being squiffy.

"I'm so pleased to see your counselling training has been worth the money." Tullene became very confused.

"But I've not had any training."

"That was sarcasm."

Pursed lips in my direction was Tullene's choice of response. As she knocked back the final drops of her mojito, we heard screams from above our heads.

"It's a zip wire!" Tullene nearly pissed her knickers. She gave me one of her *intent on partaking in an activity* looks. I knew where this was going.

"Oh no, we are not!"

For anybody who knows me well, will know that one of my biggest phobias, aside from wasps, are heights. I had discovered said fear of heights when I was a sweet sixteen year old and the London Eye had just opened. Daddy Morgan took me and my sister up on it for a New Year treat back in the year 2000.

"If the world's going to end, I want to go up and see the view from the London Eye first," my father had declared. I'm glad he had his priorities right.

In case anybody isn't aware, the London Eye is basically a massive Ferris wheel on the South Bank with 360 degree views across the capital. And it's bloody high up. We were having a lovely family day out. As we began our journey in a capsule, soaking up the sights and views from a very great height, we could see St Paul's cathedral, the OXO tower etc etc, when I suddenly came over all queer. And by queer, I don't mean I'd suddenly discovered my sexuality. That had come much earlier than my sixteenth birthday.

I felt quite nauseous and I went all dizzy. My sister grabbed me and told me to sit down with my head between my legs. I did as I was instructed but missed the rest of the journey and the spectacle of the landscape from that high up. The only view I had for the rest of the ride was my knees.

"What a waste of money bringing you on the London Eye," my dad had barked. So sympathetic. From that day, I've been petrified of anything higher than a step ladder.

But that didn't stop my so-called best friend who was fully aware of my acrophobia, that's the medical term for fear of heights BTW, dragging me to do a zip wire in Cancun.

"I can't do it", I pulled at Tullene's bikini strap to get her attention as we were being strapped into our safety belts.

"Yes you can! PMA!" I hate it when people use my own positivity slogan against me. I could feel myself starting to hyperventilate.

"Tullene!"

"I'm going to slap you in a minute. See you on the other side." And then she was away down the line. WHOOSH! I turned to the instructor.

"I'm too scared."

But my pleas fell on deaf ears. She either didn't understand English or she relished in seeing holiday makers in fear.

Before I could beg her to get me down, she gave my back a shove and I was travelling fifty feet above ground level.

"Heeeeeeelllllllp!!! Pleeeeaaassseeeeeeee!" I closed my eyes. I couldn't bear to look down.

"Dear God, please let me survive. Please save me. Don't let me die." I resorted to prayer.

Arriving at the end of the line, I finally opened my eyes as I landed on the platform and was greeted by Tullene smiling like a Cheshire cat.

"Isn't it great?" I wasn't convinced.

"I guess I'm glad I've done it. It was quite a rush even though I was shitting myself."

"Come on then", Tullene demanded, "We've got six more to complete."

I was rendered speechless for a moment.

"Hang on, for a minute there, I could have sworn you just said we had six more to do."

"I did say that." I hadn't misunderstood.

"Oh no. I've done one, that's enough for me." I started walking away, until I realised I had nowhere to go except for another ladder which seemed to go up towards another zip line.

"Good luck," I heard one of the instructors say, "you're in the middle of a jungle. There is no way out. You have to complete the course of seven."

My nostrils flared. Tullene got quite scared. I remember she turned quite pale from the fear of my *I'm going to kill you* glare, a look I saved for *very* special occasions.

"Ri…right", she stuttered. That meant said glare had achieved said outcome.

"You can ride on my back if it will help you. We can strap on to the line together."

So that's how I managed to complete this very high, very scary zip wire course; by doing my greatest impression of a tortoise, riding on

Tullene's back. She wasn't impressed some of the time as through sheer fear, I kept covering her eyes with my hands, just to ensure I had a greater grip of her.

"I would like to actually see the view when I'm fifty foot above the ground!" She yelled.

Finally at the end of the course and feeling like I'd just lost twenty years off my life, I rushed to the bar. A very handsome Mexican gentleman came up next to me. He smiled.

"Tequila?"

"I've never tried it."

"Well you should. I'll show you the proper Mexicana way!"

I then found myself licking up salt, knocking back tequila and sucking on a lemon, in that order, for about half an hour. It seemed that Mateo, that was his name, could really handle his hard liquor. Unlike myself, who could feel the room starting to spin. Well, I say room, we were by an outdoor swimming pool.

"Now," Mateo grabbed me seductively and I saw he had two heads that had suddenly appeared, "I take you back to my room to show another Mexicana tradition."

Being quite a worldly wise man, even when I'm suffering from the effects of too much tequila, I gathered he wasn't talking about showing me a patchwork quilt or a piece of Mexican artwork. I panicked that I might not even be able to get an erection after the quantity of tequila consumed. I was feeling more than just a bit squiffy.

As Mateo took my hand to lead me away from the bar, Tullene approached us.

"Where are you going?"

"Is this your wife?" Mateo enquired.

"It's alright Tullene." I could hear that that sentence had come out rather slurred.

"I'm following you to check you're okay."

Tullene is a good bodyguard. I decided against arguing the point. She is as stubborn as a mule so I knew she'd be hot on our heels whether I said no or not.

"You want more tequila?" Mateo suggested as we crossed the road to his apartment. But I couldn't make it any further. The tequila had ruined me and was now at full effect. Before I could say, O'lay!, I lost my balance and I seemed to be face down in the gutter, my cheek resting on a kerb.

Mateo whizzed off as he saw Tullene coming to my aid.

"Maybe another time!" I heard him say as he left me kissing the kerb, and wandering back to the bar. Tullene dragged me up from the road and somehow she managed to put me to bed. And ever since that day, tequila goes nowhere near my lips.

Raj (February 2020)

I don't know if what I'm about to say will be classed as racism, since I'm about to profess my preference for this certain race. But I've always preferred a darker skinned man. Specifically Asian. Give me a beautiful Indian man or Pakistani or Sri Lankan. There are certain men of these nationalities with whom I've had rendezvous, and they have always been polite, considerate and highly sexual lovers. And Raj was no exception.

I met him at a wedding reception on Valentine's Day in 2020. Such a romantic day, I hear some of you cry. But I've never thought of it as so. Perhaps it's because I've been single most of my adult life but I find Valentine's Day nothing more than a commercial money making scheme. I think you should treat your loved ones daily, not just on the 14th February.

Anyhow, let's get back to Raj. I'm not here to preach my feelings about Saint Valentine. He was the barman at this wedding (Raj, not St. Valentine) I was attending and he latched onto me as soon as he clapped eyes on me. And I certainly didn't knock back the attention. I made sure I fluttered my mascara laden eyelashes in his direction.

That's another thing I've noticed about some of my Asian lovers; they're not backward in coming forward. And Raj proved he was no exception to my rule.

As I headed towards the male bathroom to powder my nose, I saw Raj following me very intently. Perhaps the cellar is this way and he's going to change a barrel, I thought to myself as I meandered up to a urinal.

No sooner had I whipped my penis out, Raj casually strolled into the toilets. Co-incidence? I think not.

"I've been watching you all night," was his first offering.

"I noticed," I replied.

And then whilst my urethra was in mid-flow towards the urinal, Raj grabbed my face in his hands and kissed me. I looked down and noticed a bit of my piss splash about. See, I told you Valetine's Day isn't romantic.

"You could at least let me finish my business," I protested but my words seemed to fall on deaf ears.

As I went to zip up my flies, Raj gripped my hands to stop said action from happening. And then quite out of nowhere, dropped to his knees and wrapped his juicy delicate lips around my man meat. I told you he wasn't backward in coming forward.

As I started to moan and groan from Raj's actions on my downstairs department, I saw the door open but it was too late to act and push Raj away from his duties.

OH. MY. GOD. It was my brother. We said nothing. He just turned around and walked out. I think he was probably traumatised. He probably has PTSD even now. And we have never mentioned it to this day.

"Right," I sternly announced as I pulled my zipper up, "here is not the best place."

"Where then? I finish at 11."

I was staying at Tullene's this particular night as her flat happened to be closer to the wedding venue than mine so it made sense.

"Give me your number," I demanded, "I will sneak you into my best friend's flat once she's asleep."

I don't know why I didn't just ask Tullene if I could have a gentleman caller come to stay. Perhaps it seemed more exciting at the time to sneak someone in.

Now, before I continue this story of my love affair with Raj, I must inform you of some details regarding Tullene's living arrangements as they are crucial to understanding this story better. Whenever I stay over, Tullene gives me her bed and she sleeps on the sofa bed in the lounge. She's very kind like that. And you also need to know about her recycling bin. She doesn't have one. She has a carrier bag hanging on the lounge door handle where she places glass bottles and the like. Exactly why I'm regaling you with these specific facts will all become clear.

More than a little squiffy, Tullene and myself stumbled back to her flat from the wedding. I could see she was ready to collapse; she gets this glazed look in her eyes so I always know once she's far too intoxicated and needs to sleep immediately. So I started to prep for my secret mission of sneaking Raj in.

As soon as I was sure Tullene was asleep, it was time to begin project 'Get Raj In'. You can always be certain Tullene has passed out as her snoring can be heard in Australia. All the way from London.

"Ssh!" I whispered as Raj came through the front door. We tiptoed towards the bedroom when I noticed Tullene had left the lounge door open. Knowing how vocal I can be during a session of sex; I carefully went to shut it but as it came towards the doorframe…

SMASH! BANG! The recycling bag, full of wine bottles mainly, had swung against the wall and crashed and banged and clattered. I saw Tullene jolt up from her slumber.

"What's going on?" She screamed.

My reflex action pushed Raj into the bedroom with a rather hard force to make sure he was out of eyeshot. The poor man must have been so confused and probably concussed. And even potentially broke a bone.

"Nothing darling. You really should get a proper recycling bin. I was just shutting the door because your snoring was keeping me awake." Nice save. I can be a good liar in a crisis or when the need arises.

Finally having my wicked way with Raj, my sex noises seemed to be louder than usual. Probably because of the copious amounts of Savvy B consumed at the wedding.

As we frolicked under the sheets, I heard a knock at the bedroom door. That stopped me in my tracks. I looked at Raj and there was only one thing for it. I pushed him down and held his head under the duvet. And told him to hold his breath.

Not waiting for me to answer her knock, Tullene barged into the bedroom. I did another Oscar worthy performance, looking up at her, bleary eyed as if she'd just woken me from a deep sleep. My performance for the award continued.

"Wh…what?" Pretending to stutter as if I hadn't fully woken up yet.

"I heard your sex noises."

"I must have been having a wet dream", I insisted.

And luckily, she fell for my tale and left the room before Raj suffered from suffocation.

CHAPTER 20

I never thought Boris Johnson would make it into this book (March 2020)

Since Christmas of 2019, we'd been hearing about some disease in China but I hadn't really paid any attention to it. I don't think anybody really had. Why would you when it's hundreds and thousands of miles away?

It wasn't until we started hearing tales of it spreading into Europe that it made me start to sit up and take notice. And when countries like Germany and France went into something called a lockdown, I did find myself slightly on edge. New Zealand had gone into a lockdown weeks before.

Immediately I thought of Billy. When I'd heard the news I decided it was the perfect opportunity, and excuse, to send him a message. I hadn't spoken to him since the day he left for his secondment.

"If you think he's the love of your life, you should probably keep in touch," Buttplug had advised several times over the months.

"I can't. It's too painful." And that wasn't me being dramatic, like I know I am 99 percent of the time. I was genuinely trying to protect my heart by not communicating with him. Out of sight, out of mind, as the old adage goes.

Me: Oh my god. NZ in lockdown. Are you okay?

BILLY: Sorry, do I know you?

I was glad to see him being over 11,000 miles away hadn't made him lose his sarcasm and playful sense of humour. At least I hoped it was a joke and he hadn't genuinely forgotten me already. I responded appropriately.

ME: No, I found your number in a phone box and was feeling desperate.

BILLY: Ouch!

ME: So?

BILLY: It's weird. It's like something out of a science fiction movie.

ME: Are you allowed out?

BILLY: You're not meant to. Only for shopping or work etc.

ME: I bet you're lonely? And horny?

BILLY: Luckily Arthur moved in a couple of months ago so I've got company.

ME: Oh lovely. Glad you've got a lodger.

BILLY: A lodger who shares my bed.

My worst nightmare was staring back at me on a telephone screen. It hadn't even occurred to me that Arthur may have been a lover or boyfriend. I had to do my best poker face.

ME: Good for you! Serious?

BILLY: Don't know yet. Guess it must be if he's moved in.

ME: Well good luck surviving this coronavirus! Speak soon.

When the current prime minister, Boris Johnson popped up on my television screen one Sunday night to make an important announcement, I thought I had better pay attention.

BORIS: From this evening, I must give the British people a very simple instruction. You must stay at home.

My jaw dropped. I picked up my mobile.

ME: Tullene! Have you got Boris on?

TULLENE: Yes. He could have brushed his hair.

I was glued to the screen as something I'd never known to happen was unravelling before my very eyes. I knew I was witnessing history in the making.

BORIS: …these are the only reasons you should be leaving your home. You should not be meeting friends. If your friends ask you to meet, you should say no…

ME: Don't ask me Tullene.

TULLENE: Boris has just given me a good excuse to say no to seeing you now.

ME: Very funny.

BORIS: …we will close all non-essential shops…

ME: Shit. I can't work. He's just told me to close my business.

TULLENE: Fuck.

BORIS: We will beat the coronavirus and we will beat it together. I urge you at this time of national emergency to stay home, protect our NHS and save lives.

TULLENE: Well. I'll see you on the other side.

I had one major concern.

ME: How am I going to have sex?

. . .

LOCKDOWN (April/May/June 2020)

I had to stop masturbating. I was becoming far too addicted. And I was getting a bit sore if I'm honest. Not only had coronavirus put us into a situation where we were separated from our friends and families, it had also given singletons an extra problem.

I was on edge about when I could have sex again. I'm not saying I'm a slut, but I've got needs, just like the next person. I was craving a one night stand. A moment of passion. A lover. You catch the drift.

It had been almost three weeks since the enforced dry spell had been pushed upon me by Boris. I remember being so horny, I even started perving on my postman. Who is a rather balding older gentlemen with a beer belly.

To take my mind off the problem, I'd started cycling 15 miles a day. It was so eery being out and about in those first few weeks of lockdown. The streets were empty. You might see the other odd walker or cyclist on the roads or pavements but if you did, they'd cross the road to avoid you or try to stay as far away from you as possible. It was a very weird, surreal time. And it also made me perform a few actions that I may not have contemplated if we hadn't been living in covid times. Like texting a certain man, for example. WE ALL had too much time on our hands.

ME: How are you?

TRAVIS: Surviving Mr Mark! You?

ME: Weird times we're living in.

I think it was the extreme horniness that pushed me into being so forthright and sending my next text. Or it may have been the distress of having found out that Billy was living with Arthur. Or I could even blame the stress of coronavirus. Or it might just have been a combination of the three.

ME: Do you want to take me on a date once lockdown is over?

TRAVIS: Oh, you finally want to suggest some more dates to me? I did say in my last message (OVER A YEAR AGO), that I was very sorry I was so busy.

ME: But you didn't bother to arrange a second date!!!! (Exclamation marks for effect)

TRAVIS: But I told you how I genuinely felt about you. And you ignored me. I was so stressed out with work and you didn't comfort me or offer me support.

Tullene's face popped up on my Zoom. That was another thing that changed during covid. Do you remember everybody going wild about video calls? I guess it was the only "real" way that you could actually "see" your loved ones during that time.

"You're telling me that Travis HAS the HUMP with YOU?" She was really emphasising certain words to ensure she was getting her point across. "I hope you told him where to get off."

"I didn't get a chance. He told me not to bother speaking to him because he didn't want to date somebody who showed no empathy when he's stressed."

"Why the HELL did YOU even message him?" I had to tell her to stop with the accentuating of certain words. It was quite distracting.

"I don't know Tullene. I guess after seeing Billy moving on, I just. Oh, I don't know." I took a swig of my Savvy B. "I really thought me and Billy were waiting for each other."

"You've been having flings though? You didn't both take a vow of chastity for the two years he's away, did you?" She knocked back her prosecco. I hate it when Tullene has a relevant point. "Maybe Arthur is someone to kill the time. Everyone has needs."

"Time will tell, I suppose. But for now, it looks like my bridges with both of them are burnt." And then I poured myself another large glass of plonk.

It wasn't just me and Tullene whom had become accustomed to a video chat during lockdown. I'd been having game and quiz nights via Zoom with Buttplug. But getting Mummy Morgan to muster the art of a live video call proved a harder task. As she is classed as vulnerable, due to various medical ailments, I was out and about doing shopping for my mum and dad and dropping it in to them. And by this point, you were allowed your "bubble"- at least that's what the government were calling it. Remember some of the contradictory, bat shit crazy rules they kept coming up with?

You could see someone out of your household, OUTDOORS, as long as you stayed two metres apart. So I visited Mummy and Daddy Morgan in their garden.

"Grandad! Grandad!" I heard my mum bellow as I walked up their garden path, shopping bags in each hand on this one particular morning. Ever since my nephews have come along, my mother and father don't seem to have first names for each other anymore. It's always Nana or Grandad.

"Mum." I said as I placed the bags on the patio and stepped two metres back. My maths has never been the greatest so Daddy Morgan had put lines all over the garden with masking tape to indicate two metres. Very handy to ensure we maintained the correct distance. And very infuriating if you accidentally stepped over one of his markers as he would yell, "GET BACK!" As you can see, it's not just me who is dramatic. It's a family trait in the genes.

"I wish I could give you a great big hug." My mum looked sad.

"You will be able to soon," I assured her. "But at least I get to see you in the garden."

"I feel like a bleeding prisoner on visiting day. I put you a glass of wine on the table. It's New Zealand." Even though she only ever buys me sauvignon blanc from this particular country, she still feels the need to tell me where it's from every time she pours me a drink.

"Mother, it's only 2pm!" But who was I kidding? I lifted up the glass and took a big gulp.

"You don't have to drink it you know." Sarcasm runs in my family too.

"It's a shame to waste it!" I said, justifying my actions. And that's another thing everyone will recall about covid restrictions. The majority of the population became alcoholics.

"I bet dad's already on the sauce."

"Don't talk to me about your bleeding father."

"Oh god. What's he done now?"

"He's been on that Stella since midday. I said to him, I said, you drink all that beer and it won't be the bloody corona you'll have to worry about. It'll be liver failure."

"Mum. These are strange times. He needs to let his hair down a bit."

"He ain't got no hair, has he?" I momentarily forgot that fact. I don't know how I could, considering I am now as bald as a newborn. And it's probably his fault. Genetics again. My family's genes have made me dramatic, sarcastic and bald. Great.

"It was mayhem in Morrisons. It's like a Saturday night at a Soho club. One in, one out door policy to restrict numbers inside."

"That's what your Aunty Sue said about Sainsburys."

I was flabbergasted. Aunty Sue was eighty at the time.

"Don't she know she should be staying at home?"

"You know what a stubborn old bitch she is, Mark," my mum is quite fond of her sister, although you wouldn't know it to hear her talk about her. "I said that to her but do you know what she said?"

"What?"

"She goes, I've survived Hitler, two heart attacks and a hip replacement."

Fair, fair point. Aunty Sue is like a cat with nine lives.

"Did you manage to get any loo roll?" Her next question.

Who remembers the madness of the panic buying twats that led to the shortage of toilet rolls on the supermarket shelves? It got to the point where I was having to ration the paper so I was only using one square at a time to wipe my bum. And having IBS, that was no mean feat. Desperate times.

"Have you been having video calls with the boys?"

"Of course I have. Give me a buzz every couple of days to speak to their old Nana, don't they?" I could see my mum start to fill up, her eyes looked wet.

"Mum."

"What?"

"Please don't cry."

"Oh, I just, you know, I'm glad I can see them on a video screen. But it's not the same as getting a hug from them in the flesh, is it?"

"Yeah, but you can't mum. You know you're in the high risk group."

"But they're my grandchildren!"

I was trying to be brave for Mummy Morgan's sake but I felt the same. I did miss physical contact during those bloody lockdowns. Just a simple hug from my mum or my nephews. I didn't realise how important it was until that time.

It got to May and I think I'd exhausted the videos on Pornhub. I'd watched their whole back catalogue. And Only Dudes. And most of the other porn sites on the internet.

ME: I'm really sorry if you think I didn't respond in the manner I should have. Maybe I should have been more sympathetic. Are you still stressed at work?

TRAVIS: I quit. I'm no longer a train driver. I drive an HGV lorry around the country now. And apology accepted.

ME: I've always wondered what we might have become after that date. I'd like to see more of you.

TRAVIS: Well, I promise you will. As soon as lockdown is over.

ME: But why wait until then?

TRAVIS: Oh no, I couldn't break the rules, sorry.

ME: But you can see MORE of me without meeting in the flesh. 😉

And then a dick pic appeared in my inbox. Apart from the time Travis randomly turned up as the stripper at my thirtieth birthday bash, I'd never clapped eyes on his penis. Especially not in an erect state.

And before you could scream, *UP THE BUM AND NO BABIES,* Travis and I became addicted to video sex on a regular basis. And that's how I survived the rest of the first lockdown. I didn't do so well in the next lockdown. But more of that later.

CHAPTER 21

Travis and his lorry (July 2020)

I remember the day lockdown was lifted. It felt such a relief to be able to go to work and see people again. But my main concern was finding some male company in the bedroom again.

After some amazing 'sex' with Travis via Zoom, I hoped and prayed that the intercourse would be just as mind blowing in the flesh.

TRAVIS: Can you see the big lorry from your bedroom window?

I grappled with my net curtains and saw an HGV parked up in a bay across the road. AND YES, I do still have net curtains up in my flat. AND ALSO YES, I am fully aware it is no longer 1980.

ME: Have you got surveillance cameras on my street?

TRAVIS: There's more than enough room in the back for you to come join me…

I knew exactly what the DOT DOT DOT was an indicator of. I'd never seen myself move so fast.

ME: This is definitely your lorry? I don't want to be kidnapped and smuggled out of the country.

TRAVIS: YES! Get outside. I've left the roller door at the back slightly ajar for you so you can sneak in.

Rushing out of my front door, I headed towards Travis's truck. I suddenly got a flash of nerves in the pit of my stomach. Yes, I'd been having regular 'Zoom sex' with him but this was to be the first time in real life.

What if it wasn't good?

What if we don't like it in reality with each other?

And why are we doing it in the back of a lorry when my flat is just up there?

But I ignored the latter question in my head and came to the conclusion that this was a bit of excitement and something a little bit daring. I enjoyed the spontaneity.

I used my inner Tullene to give myself a good stern talking to. *If you don't get your arse in the back of the lorry, you'll never find out.*

I got to the back of his vehicle and indeed, he had left his back flap slightly ajar. Yes, I know that sounds slightly innuendo-ISH. Actually, NOT slightly. It sounds like a massive innuendo.

Until that moment, I never knew I had gymnastic genes as I Roly polyed into the back of the HGV. Perhaps my grandma was an acrobat or part of a travelling circus troupe.

As quickly as I had performed my gymnastics and was safely inside the back of his truck, Travis had his flap pulled and locked shut.

"Did anyone see you?" He sounded panicked.

"I didn't have time to look."

We shared an awkward moment, just smiling at each other. It was clear to see that we were both extremely nervous. He looked me up and down, surveying the scene, clearly so pleased to see me. Twenty years since I'd first clapped eyes on this man. Twenty years of missed opportunities. Twenty years of never truly making it work.

His breathing sounded heavy, nervous. I broke the tension by grabbing his body and pulling it in close to me. His heart was beating fast. Faster than I'd ever heard anybody's beat. I prayed he wouldn't have a heart attack before I'd had my field watered. There had been a drought during covid. Okay, maybe that wasn't one of my best euphemisms.

Travis released himself from my grip and looked straight into my blue eyes. He leant into my lips and placed his on mine. I'd never known a kiss quite like it. It felt so passionate but edgy all at once, like it was the first time he'd ever kissed anybody.

But after the initial anxiety, it didn't take us much longer to warm up to the main event. As soon as I reciprocated the kiss, he became more like the video sex Travis I'd come to know and worship. Naughty, sensual but tentative.

We ripped each other's clothes off like we were competing to get into the world record books. And made love. Pure, unadulterated love making.

As penetration was in full force, Travis stopped my thrusting for a second.

"Do you think the lorry is shaking?" His voice panting.

"Who cares?" I was eager to get back to my hole. Well, not mine technically. His.

"Perhaps you better not drive with such robust force."

Travis had always had a way with his words. The pun hadn't escaped me but I was far too engaged in my first sexual act in months. Plus the fact it was with a man who I had waited twenty years to make love to.

It took us a long time to finally reach that moment. The ups and downs; the feeling of Travis being my soulmate but then him disappointing me on numerous occasions. I believed in that moment that perhaps he was my one true love, the one everybody talks about. The sex was great and I remember thinking, Travis is my one for life now. But that didn't stop me thinking of Billy for a split second.

I hadn't forgotten the feelings I felt for Billy. I could imagine marrying him. My inner saboteur arrived on my shoulder.

Could I imagine marrying Travis?

Was there too much water under our bridge?

I decided I needed to stop procrastinating. Billy was over 11,000 miles away living with Arthur, whom I had decided was an arsehole. I mean, I didn't even know this bloke but jealousy makes you bitter and I believed he was an a-hole for stealing Billy from me.

As I reached climax, Travis screamed out some words which stopped my overactive thoughts in their tracks.

"I LOVE YOU MR MARK!"

You're not sick, you're just in love (August 2020)

I'd started walking around like I was a part in a romantic film on Netflix. I found myself walking taller, head held high and strutting down the street like I was a catwalk model.

I heard singing but there was no-one there. I smelt blossom but the trees were bare. (Okay, it was the height of summer but just join me on this pleasant journey of describing my feelings.)

All day long, I seemed to walk on air. I wondered why but I knew exactly what had caused my mood. Travis had declared he loved me. The man who had first turned up in a gay nightclub in the early noughties had finally confessed his undying love for me. And made it official by actually spending most of his waking hours with me.

And also his sleeping hours as he seemed to have unofficially moved into my flat.

And what's more, I'd lost my appetite. Which for anybody who knows me and my love affair with food, will find absolutely shocking.

Stars that usually twinkled in the sky were also twinkling in my eyes. And that happened everytime I saw or thought about Travis. For the first time in my whole adult life, I actually wanted to spend quality time with a man. Not just use them for a quick shag and then kick them out.

"What's wrong with me Tullene? I can't concentrate."

"Listen love, you don't need analysing. It's not surprising."

"I feel very strange but nice. My heart keeps going pitter patter, like so fast. Do you think I need to see a doctor?"

"No. I know just what's the matter. There is nothing you can take. You're not sick, you're just in love."

And she was absolutely spot on. Hit the nail on the head like a carpenter.

"Right, so when are we going to meet him?" Tullene enquired.

"But you know him."

"Oh yes, but not properly. I want to be introduced to him as your boyfriend. And so will Sarah."

"Whose Sarah?" I sometimes momentarily forget Buttplug actually has a real name.

And so I did as I was told and arranged dinner for the four of us.

Tullene and Buttplug were both unfashionably early for the dinner party I had arranged. They were so early in fact, that I hadn't even finished cooking when they graced my flat doorstep. And the guest of honour, AKA Travis wasn't even on the premises yet.

But it was rather fortunate that they had arrived before my beau. It gave me a chance to lay down some ground rules to the pair.

"Right. No Spanish inquisition. No interrogation tactics like MI5," I warned them as I handed over alcoholic beverages.

The pair looked at each other and it was almost as though they had planned a script together.

"We'll only get the thumb screws out if it's absolutely necessary." It's lucky I knew they were joking. Although with Tullene it isn't always so easy to tell as her delivery is so deadpan.

"And no acting like my mum." That was the final warning time would allow as the doorbell went as soon as the words left my mouth. No-one moved for a moment.

"Well go and let him in then." Tullene gestured me towards the door.

"I don't know why he's ringing the bell; he's got a spare set of keys."

I opened the door and Travis looked more handsome than ever. Everytime I saw him, I still got butterflies. My stomach flipped and high kicked as he kissed me on the lips. A rather long, lingering smooch. So long and lingering that we were interrupted by a loud booming voice. It was Tullene.

"We'll have none of that behaviour in here. This is a civilised apartment."

Travis broke away from our kiss and before I could re-introduce them, he had his arms flung around her.

"I haven't seen you in years!" came Travis's reply.

"Ten years actually. When I saw rather a lot of you as you stripped your clothes off."

She indicated exactly what she saw by gesturing her eyes down towards his penis. I slapped her arm.

"You haven't changed a bit. Still as attractive as ever."

Tullene's head swelled and I saw her gloating face appear. Not very good at acting humble is Tullene.

"Oh Mark! He can stay. When was the last time you said anything like that to me, you bastard?"

And she faux dramatically slapped me across the back for effect. Although not so faux as the movement jolted me and my Savvy B splashed onto the carpet. Tullene attempted to distract from the situation.

"You remember Buttplug?"

"Does he still call you that god awful nickname darling?"

"Yes he does."

"Oh you love it." I Informed her.

Travis wrapped his arms around the other dinner guest and planted a kiss on each of her cheeks. Very continental.

"You can call me Sarah."

I interrupted the formalities as dinner was about to burn.

"Let's all take our seats."

"Oh great. I'm starving." All the guests declared.

Travis glanced over at me, smiled and winked. I caught a glimpse of an exchange between Tullene and Buttplug – I could tell they approved.

Sitting around the dinner table, I'd laid it with tulips and candles aplenty to set the ambience. Everybody began tucking into my five star cuisine. Okay, so that's sarcasm. My cooking would win no awards as I'm a typical British 'man' cook. I can cook enough to not starve but nothing fancy ever comes out of my kitchen.

My signature dishes include:

Sausage casserole

Coq au vin (yes, sounds quite fancy but is just a chicken casserole)

Spaghetti Bolognese

Lasagne

Paneer curry

And not forgetting my offering for this particular evening, Hunter's chicken with cheesy mash and broccoli.

Topping up my guest's wine glasses, they were busily tucking into my culinary delight. Until Tullene decided it was time to start the interrogations.

"So what are your intentions Travis? Are you serious about Mark? It took you long enough to get your act together."

Cue awkward silence. I heard Travis gulp. Buttplug's knife and fork nervously cut into her chicken. And Tullene just took a swig of her wine as though she'd only asked if he was going on holiday that year. Meanwhile, I pursed my lips in her direction and took a sharp intake of breath.

"Very subtle Tullene."

I grabbed Travis's hand to comfort him. I don't know why I thought he might need comforting, it's not like anybody had just died. But I know what it can be like to be on the end of Tullene's interrogations.

"You don't need to answer that."

"Yes he does."

Tullene was lucky she wasn't sat directly across from me. She'd escaped from my being able to kick her under the table. Travis took a rather large swig of Savvy B. Dutch courage. And then began his explanation.

"I wasn't in a good place for the last couple of years. My job was stressful, I had trouble focussing on myself, let alone somebody else. But now I've got a new job, it's less stressful and I have more time to look after myself. Which means I can dedicate more time to Mark. I love him so much. I think I've actually loved him since we first met in that gay club all those years ago. But it was just never the right time. I think I always knew deep within my heart that we would end up together. Somehow."

Cue speechless Tullene. I don't think she'd expected such a deep, heartfelt reply to her cross-examination.

I saw Buttplug wipe a tear from her eye. I had a lump in my throat. And it wasn't because I had overcooked my chicken and dried it out. Travis gripped my hand. And Tullene nodded approvingly. "How's everybody's dinner?" I inquired.

My three guests glanced at each other, saying nothing.

"Well?"

They seemed to nod towards each other in agreement, before they spoke in unison:

"It's a bit dry!"

Bastards. I re-filled their glasses and reminded them I was no Nigella Lawson.

CHAPTER 22

A romantic mini-break; it must be true love (September 2020)

I felt like I was in a scene from Chitty Chitty Bang Bang as we made our way to our first ever mini-break together. I'm not quite sure why I imagined I was in that particular film. My car wasn't flying in the air towards our destination. But I guess it was a euphemism for how I was floating and in love.

We were headed towards the Jurassic Coast in Dorset. If you haven't been, you really must put it on your bucket list. The scenery is breathtaking. And when I say breathtaking, walking up and down the steep cliffs literally takes your breath away. Travis had to push me up at one point because I thought I wouldn't make it to the top.

We arrived at our little holiday cottage we had booked and it was a little barn conversion. All wooden slats, complete with an old barn door still.

"This is perfect!" I yelped as Travis picked me up and carried me over the threshold. "We're not even married yet!"

"Yes, I know we're not," he said, dumping me on the bed, bead of sweat developing on his forehead. I think I was heavier than he had imagined. "But it's our first ever holiday together so I wanted to make the gesture."

I kept thinking somebody was going to pinch me any minute and awaken me from this dream. But I gripped Travis's face tight in my hands and knew it was no fantasy. This man in front of my eyes had chosen me. My soulmate.

"What are you smiling at?" Travis questioned as he clocked my Cheshire cat impression.

"I know it took twenty years for us to finally get our act together but I'm just so happy it's happened at long last."

"What's meant for you, won't pass you by." Very philosophical of Travis.

"It kept passing me by a fucking lot over the years." We both laughed. And then we made love. We had to christen the barn after all. It was the decent thing to do.

After that particular session of love making was complete, we decided to go for a walk along some of the coast. We held hands as we made our way to the top of this particular cliff. I could see Travis becoming a little breathless. He stopped for a moment, looking uncharacteristically worried. He could see the concern spread across my face.

"Don't panic Mr Mark. I'm just not used to walking these cliffs. We don't have many of them in London, do we?" And I noticed him clutch his chest slightly as he reassured me.

"Sit down for a minute," I wasn't taking no for an answer. "Have you a pain in your chest?"

"Stop fussing. It's just beating faster because we've done a bloody great hike up this monster cliff."

We finally made it to the top without either of us collapsing. Travis was right, two London boys weren't used to such a hilly domain.

The view actually brought a tear to my eye. At that moment in time, I thought life couldn't get much more perfect. Travis's hand was in mine. The sun was setting. And all you could see for miles around was the southern coast line. I felt I had died and gone to heaven.

"Let's just sit here and watch the sun go down." I wasn't going to argue with that suggestion from my holiday companion.

We nestled down on the grassy verge and I rested my head on Travis's chest. He tentatively stroked my bald slaphead and I could hear the beating of his heart. It did seem abnormally fast but I figured it was just the over exertion from the walk.

He glanced down at me as I made myself comfortable on his pectoralis major and his eyes glistened. That was the look of a man who loved you. I could tell. I could have cried with happiness. Or burst with joy. Or just cartwheeled with contentment. He pecked me on the lips as the sun set.

"Here's to the rest of our lives together Mr Mark." A lump appeared in my throat. And I could hear his voice crack as though he might burst into tears of overwhelming emotion.

"I love you Mr Travis!"

CHAPTER 23

Skinnydipping- That time a dog ran away with our clothes (The next day)

As we strolled along a secluded beach, deep within one of the Jurassic Coast's coves, Travis squeezed my hand tight. I stopped and turned on my heels to face him.

"What was that for?"

"I got a surge of love that run all through my body and I just wanted to squeeze you and pull you in so tight."

I remember in those first few months with Travis, I had never cried so much. But not because he was a nasty bastard to me. They were happy tears. My eyes would fill up because I couldn't believe how lucky I was.

"It's a shame we didn't bring our trunks with us," I said, dipping a toe in the ocean as I looked out onto the horizon. It was so peaceful.

"Who needs trunks?" Travis asked with a naughty glint in his eye. Catching on to his intention, I protested.

"Oh no. I couldn't. What if we get caught?"

"There's no one around." He'd won me over quickly. Before you could scream SPLASH, our clothes were on the rocks and our naked bodies were in the sea. It felt so liberating. Once I'd recovered from the shock of the cold. And my penis had turned into a vagina as it shrivelled up from the icy water.

As we romantically cuddled up to each other to keep warm, bobbing up and down on the waves, I noticed a dog near the shoreline. And if there were a dog, I knew a dog owner had to be nearby. Little did I realise that it was the dog we would have to be more concerned about.

"What if she sees us?" I panicked. I don't know what made me think the so far unseen dog walker was a female.

"If she sees us, she'll see two men having a dip in the Atlantic. She can't see below our chest", Travis reassured me. I've always been a scaredy cat since birth. Never really been a dare devil.

I noticed the dog having a good old sniff around our pile of clothes. Why do dogs sniff and lick everything? I guess it's in their nature. Instinctive.

And then as owner of sniffing dog came into our eyeline on the beach, my instincts of being terribly polite kicked in and I gave her a wave as I bobbed up and down on the sea.

"Talk about drawing attention to us," Travis joked, mocking my manners.

"I don't know why I did that."

But the dog mummy reciprocated my good manners and returned my gesture. Little did we know at that point what mischief her dog was responsible for.

"I need to get out in a minute before my balls drop off," I shared with the man who had turned my world upside down.

"Just let that lady get a little bit further along the shore and then we'll run over to our clothes."

As she disappeared from sight, we made a dash for the sand. My nipples could have taken someone's eye out, they were so erect.

My eyes widened and my jaw dropped as I looked down at the rocks where, at one point, there had been two full sets of clothes laid out. This was no longer the case.

"The little shit!" I bellowed.

"What's happened?"

"I'll tell you what's happened. That dog has stolen most of our clothes."

I had one sock, a t-shirt and a scarf. Travis had boxer shorts and his cardigan. Somehow we managed to cover our modesty with what was left from the dog thief and scurried back to our cottage. But we didn't half get some looks as we headed over the cliffs.

CHAPTER 24

The heart attack (November 2020)

I didn't just have sex anymore. Oh no. It was love making every-time now. And on a regular basis. Sometimes at least three times a day. I remember one particular day after the third time of penetration, Travis was particularly sore. But I'd been ready for round four, so he begged me to give him a day off. Maybe I have a sex addiction. We had been at it like rabbits for months. We were still in the honeymoon period of our relationship after all.

This one morning, I was feeling particular frisky and I saw Travis try to sneak out of the bed as he caught the passionate look in my eye.

"Just a quick one before breakfast?" I begged.

"Make it quick!"

"Oh. And who says romance is dead?"

Little did I know in that moment that those words would be the last words Travis would ever hear from my mouth. Romance, for him, did seem to cause his death.

I began penetrating and I could hear Travis becoming slightly more breathless than usual. I must be getting better in my old age, I thought, rather proudly, of my sexual abilities.

And then I saw Travis clutch his chest and become awfully pale. White as a ghost. I stopped mid-thrust. He collapsed back on the bed and didn't move a muscle.

"Travis! Travis!" I thought he was being playful at first, an excuse to get out of making love.

"Stop mucking about!" But he wasn't playing tricks. I quickly pulled out and never had I seen one of my erections deplete so fast.

I grabbed his wrist to check his pulse. I could see his chest wasn't moving. He wasn't breathing. He had no pulse.

"TRAVIS!" I began to shake and I felt a tear stream down one side of my face. It couldn't be real. He couldn't be dead.

I grappled for my mobile phone and tapped 999 onto the screen.

"Emergency. Which service please?"

"My boyfriend. I think he's dead."

"You need an ambulance?"

"I don't think you can save him"

Sitting in the family and friends room at the hospital, I was all alone. I noticed how eerily quiet it was. I don't know what I expected, what with it being a hospital. A disco? I guess I shouldn't have been shocked. But I wanted some noise. Needed it.

"Have you got any news?" I practically ripped the doctor's shirt from his back as he walked in.

"Perhaps you'd like to sit down."

"NO. I'll stand."

"We did all we could for your boyfriend but it was just too late. I'm so sorry for your loss."

I mean, I already knew he was dead in the bed. But until it was confirmed by a medical professional, I still had had some hope he wasn't. But it was real. I couldn't deny it any longer. I put my hands to my face, covering it, in case I broke down in tears but I didn't. I somehow retained my composure. I swallowed hard to be enable me to speak.

"How doctor? He's my age. So young."

"He had a cardiac arrest. I'm so sorry. It looks like he had another one, maybe a couple of months ago. But it's too early to confirm that yet."

That added piece of information floored me. And then it hit me like a lightning bolt. Travis clutching his chest as we walked in the Jurassic Coast.

"He's not coming back, is he?"

The doctor shook his head.

"Perhaps you should call a friend or family member. You should have someone with you." And, with that, the doctor left the room.

Tullene bowled into the waiting room. I'd never seen her move so quickly. A friendship of over two decades allows you to know when something is wrong. And she knew now. I hadn't been able to say it over the telephone or bring myself to tell her what happened. I just told her to get to the hospital.

"What's going on?"

I swallowed. I knew as soon as the words left me, I would break. There's only a couple of people in my life who I can cry in front of and Tullene is one of them.

"Travis," I gulped again, my voice beginning to break, "is dead."

Tullene put her hand to her mouth, shocked. She was taken aback for a moment.

"Oh Mark."

She had her arms open and ready. She knew I was going to need to be in them any minute.

And then I let out a cry. It echoed through the hospital. And Tullene pulled me in close to her chest and stroked my bald head. I saw my tears drip onto her faux leather trousers.

"Let it out." And I did. I don't remember how long I was resting on her boobs but my arm had gone to sleep by the time I pulled away from her grip.

The breakdown (January/February 2021)

Another Covid lockdown had been announced just before Christmas so it was back to being alone in my flat. The first lockdown hadn't been too bad. The weather was hot and the nights were bright. But it was the dead of winter for these new restrictions so all felt gloomy and dark and repressive.

We'd buried Travis in a lovely little service at the local church. I'd cried more on that day than I even knew was possible. I'm surprised I wasn't dehydrated for weeks afterwards, the amount of tears that left my body.

I'd not been doing any Zoom calls with Tullene or Buttplug during this lockdown. I hadn't wanted to be sociable, if I'm honest.

TULLENE: I miss you.

ME: I miss you too.

TULLENE: Zoom call tonight?

ME: I'm going to have an early night.

That was a complete lie. If truth be told, I hadn't really slept properly since Travis died. And now the new covid rules had been forced upon us, I slept even less.

I'd get into bed with the intention of falling asleep but then I would feel my heart beating faster. I'd struggle to catch my breath. And I'd get sweat all over my forehead and back. I'd have to rush out of the bed because I couldn't relax and I thought I was going to be sick.

I spent months pacing my room at night- this became a regular occurrence as part of my sleep routine. After some google searches, I came to the conclusion that I was suffering with panic attacks. Or night-time terrors.

BUTTPLUG: Games night online tonight?

ME: There's a film I want to watch.

BUTTPLUG: Tomorrow night?

ME: I'll let you know.

I don't know why I didn't tell my two best friends that I was not okay. I just didn't like the thought of anybody thinking I had any problems. Until this point, I'd always been the happy go lucky gay boy from the suburbs. And I guess that's the reputation I wanted to maintain.

It got to February and I still hadn't slept properly. I was starting to feel exhausted. I'd get into bed, feeling perfectly fine and soon after, I'd feel breathless or get a hot flush or think I would throw up. So up I'd get and I'd spend the next hour pacing. How my carpet didn't get holes in it during this time, I'll never know.

I felt worthless at this time. Covid restrictions meant we couldn't see our loved ones. It also meant I couldn't work. And I've worked since the day I was thirteen so to have that taken away from me made me feel that me and my industry and career were disposable.

Yes, I hear you cry- I've worked since I was a mere teenager. Obviously you couldn't start work that young in this day and age. You have to be 16 or even 18 to get a job now I think. But my mum kicked me out of the car and made me walk up and down the high street, asking about Saturday jobs.

I finally found one in a bakery and I loved it. Serving breakfasts, chatting to the punters. And you could also eat leftover cakes- which is probably why I was a fat teenager. I'd gut bash the lot at the end of the working day. Hence the nickname I was christened with at school- TANK.

This one particular night, no matter how much I paced, I couldn't escape my panic attack. I was practising breathing techniques I'd found on YouTube but nothing was working. I was so tired, I thought I was going mad.

I found myself sat on my bed, rocking back and forth, biting my nails. I don't know how many hours I was sat there like that. It seemed like an eternity.

ME: I'm not okay.

I was getting ready to send a text to Tullene. But I deleted it.

I told myself that I simply must say something now. Rocking on your bed is not normal behaviour. I knew I had to get help.

I grabbed my car keys from the side and got into my car. I hadn't even looked at the clock so I had no clue what time it was. But I knew where I was heading. To Tullene.

Ringing her doorbell, I noticed it was 2am. There was no answer to begin with so I rang again. That did the trick as I saw a light being turned on.

"Who is it?" I heard her shout.

"Me."

"Mark? Do you know what bloody time it is?" She bellowed as she opened the door. But she stopped screaming as soon as she took one look at me.

"Oh my god. What's happened to you?"

I walked in and couldn't speak.

"Tullene," I managed to say. But that's the only word that had a chance to leave my lips. I collapsed to the floor, crying and rocking on her carpet. I think she thought at first it was a practical joke. After all, we are renowned for being rather dramatic.

"Get up you silly bastard and tell me why you're knocking on my door at this unsightly hour!"

But I didn't move. And I didn't stop crying. Or rocking. It dawned on her that this was no pantomime.

"Oh my god." I remember her voice cracking as she realised I wasn't okay. "Come on, it's all going to be alright." She whispered softly in my ear as she grabbed my arm to get me off the floor.

"I'm sorry." That was all I could manage to say as she walked me to the sofa to sit me down.

"You don't need to be…" But she couldn't finish her sentence. I saw her fighting back her own tears. She managed to draw a sharp intake of breath, to ensure she could finish her sentence without breaking down herself. "We're going to get you to a doctor and you will be fine."

CHAPTER 25

Therapy and a rendezvous with an older gentleman (March/April 2021)

Tullene fought to keep me from being admitted to a mental health unit the night I arrived on her doorstep.

"He is staying with me. I'll make sure he's not alone."

And day by day, with the help of my therapist Will, I started to return to the Mark I knew and loved. I was fully aware I would never be the same again. After all, I'd lost the love of my life and soulmate at such a young age and at such an early stage in our relationship. And in such a soap opera-esq style.

I often wondered if Travis regretted the length of time it took him to get his act together and finally embark on a life with me. Who knows the answer to that question? I'd never know because I can't talk to dead people. Well, I don't think I possess that particular power anyway.

We were still in the midst of another bloody lockdown too. That had contributed to my breakdown, I had no doubt. Having to close my business and be told that I couldn't trade made me feel incredibly worthless. The government were basically saying my industry wasn't needed. Well, that's how I took it anyway.

"As soon as lockdown is over, I think you need a good fuck." That wasn't the advice of my therapist but Tullene. The only issue of staying with her for this period of time was we both have too much fondness for a glass of Savvy B.

Will had advised me against partaking in alcoholic beverages whilst I was recovering and in therapy but I chose to ignore that particular piece of advice. I'd had no panic attacks for weeks; I still wasn't sleeping the best but I felt much calmer, less anxious and happier staying with my best friend. I knew I was going to be okay now.

As April began, it was announced by Boris, who I was now referring to as a bastard, that covid restrictions were being lifted. I cheered as I heard the announcement on the radio.

"It's time!" I announced to Tullene that evening. She got up to go to the fridge, thinking I meant wine o'clock.

"I'll get the glasses."

"No. I mean, it's time I go back to my own flat."

She looked almost heartbroken. I think she'd enjoyed having me, albeit under rather dark circumstances.

"I think you're ready," she nodded. Looking me up and down, she inspected me like a parent sending their child to school for their first day.

"And the first thing I'm going to do is…"

"Get laid!" She finished my sentence but she was rather taken aback when I informed her she was in fact wrong with her suggestion.

"No. Book a theatre ticket. I really want to see a show."

So that's what I did. I forget what show I went to see but I boldly went on my own. I think it was something I needed to do to prove to myself I was me again. To be brave enough to enter the world alone.

I took my seat in the auditorium, clutching a glass of wine. I don't know about anyone else but I can't frequent the theatre without a beverage in my hand. It's part of my theatre tradition.

There was an older gentleman in the seat next to mine. I'd glanced at him for a moment, thinking he looked like he was on his own too. But then I took my seat, excited to have a swig of Savvy B, so didn't give him anymore thought. Until…

"Oooh, you've given me the taste for a glass of wine too." This random voice boomed in my ear and startled me. It came from said man in the seat next to mine.

"Oh yes", I agreed, "you can't come to a show without partaking in one. You've got ten minutes until curtain up, go and get yourself one." I know, I'm a bad influence. Even to strangers.

"You've twisted my arm", he responded in a rather camp manner as he stood up. He was definitely a fellow poofter.

"What's your poison?" He enquired, pointing towards the drink in my hand.

"Savvy B," I quickly answered, "from the Marlborough region."

"A man after my own heart!" His voice echoed across the stalls. He must be on the stage, I thought. And off he went to the bar, returning with two glasses in his hands.

"I thought I was a lush!" I cheekily joked.

"One's for you," he informed me, plonking the second glass next to my foot.

"That's very kind."

ME: A man sat next to me. Blatantly trying to get me into bed. About 60!!!

TULLENE: *You're blatantly going to shag him.*

ME: *I think he's a bit old. Even for me.*

As the show finished, the company took their bows and as the curtain came down, I stood up and smiled at my companion next to me.

"Lovely to meet you..." It suddenly dawned on me that I didn't even know his name.

"I'm Alan," he introduced himself, standing up and putting out his hand for me to shake. "I'm only staying up the road, in a lovely hotel. Would you like to come for a late dinner?"

"Are you actually inviting me for dinner? Or is that code for something else?" I think he was impressed with my bluntness. It's a talent I possess that has put many men off over the years. But clearly not this one.

"I had to make it sound like I wasn't just trying to get you into bed."

"Even though you are." We both laughed. "How old are you anyway?"

"It's rude to ask a lady her age", he retorted.

"I don't see no lady." I was quick on my heels with that one.

"Sixty one." I think he expected me to run for the hills once he'd announced his age. "If that bothers you, let's go our separate ways now."

"My mum has always taught me to do the occasional bit of charity work so it's your lucky night!"

"You cheeky little shit!" But my cheek hadn't put him off. As if by magic, we were in his hotel room and he was suddenly sucking me off. Of course we hadn't arrived there by any spell, we had just walked up the road.

Until that evening, I'd never slept with someone that much older than me. But there were definitely no regrets. There is a lot to be said for going to bed with an older man. They certainly have experience when it comes to such matters. Well, Alan sure did anyway.

CHAPTER 26

With age comes experience. With youth comes enthusiasm. (May 2021)

After the experience of sleeping with an older man, I made the decision that I would stick to the older age bracket. But that didn't last for long. My next encounter involved a younger man. At least no-one can accuse me of being ageist.

We were out for dinner one night in a lovely little bistro; when I say WE, you can make an educated guess as to whom I was with, can't you?

"Prosecco anyone?" Tullene asked, although it was more of a statement than a question. We WERE having prosecco because she had decided.

As the waiter approached our table, my jaw hit the deck. O-M-G. In front of my eyes was the most beautiful Sri Lankan male, complete with a peachy bum and the body of someone who definitely had a twenty hour gym membership.

He winked at me as he asked for our drinks order and I noticed his teeth dazzle both me and my dinner companion. Walking off to attend to our prosecco, I gripped Tullene's arm tightly.

"He winked at me."

"He probably had something in his eye."

BITCH.

"I'm in love."

"Here we go again."

DOUBLE BITCH.

"I'm just glad I'm back in the saddle."

She placed her hand on top of mine.

"Me too. I was worried you'd lost the plot a few months ago."

"You can't keep Mark Morgan down for long…" I declared.

"…Unless he's giving a blow job!" Tullene finished my sentence. She knows me so well.

Ravi arrived with our sparkling plonk. Yes, Ravi. I had already found out his name. He was 29. Yes, 29. I had also found out his age. And he was single. Yes, single. I'd also found out his dating status.

And yes, he was free to come back to mine after his shift that night because I had already asked him that too. After Travis and then my breakdown, it had made me come to the conclusion that you can't wait around. Life is not a dress rehearsal. And it is too short to mess about. And sex is there to enjoy.

Meal complete. Tullene was put in an uber. And Ravi was just walking into my flat. He planted his lips on mine before I even had a chance to close the front door. He kissed me like he was on drugs. So fast and passionate. Albeit a bit sloppy too.

I soon learnt the difference in sex with two different age brackets. With age comes experience. With youth comes enthusiasm. I preferred both. Now my task was to track down a man who encompassed both these qualities.

I pulled down Ravi's trousers to perform one of my famous blow jobs. Well, I think they're famous. Unzipping his flies, I was nearly poked in the eye with his rather large brown instrument. And it certainly wasn't a flute, let me assure you of that. More of a clarinet. And yes, there was also a bend at the end.

So much so, that I thought I may get whiplash from sucking it. And after a while, I started feeling a bit dizzy. But I needn't have worried, as he didn't last very long, because something else about sleeping with a younger gentleman; they cum so quickly.

Pulling his trousers back up, I took a sip of water and asked when I could see him again.

"I am going away for two weeks to get married..."

I almost spat out my H20.

"...But I could see you again when I come back."

I leapt up from the bed. That is one territory I never trespass on-married or taken men.

"I don't think so," I replied. "Your poor husband. You shouldn't even be here tonight. You told me you were single."

"I am single." Perhaps the prosecco had frazzled my brain as I was struggling to keep up with the confusing conversation. But then he provided me with some more clarity on the situation. "It is an arranged marriage in Sri Lanka with a woman. But then I'm coming back to London and she will stay there."

I pondered for a moment. Maybe I could see him again then. But then I decided no, it would all end in tears, I told myself. We could never be out in the open if his whole family and friends think he's married, to a woman! I had decided at a young age that I would never be anybody's dirty little secret.

"I think you should leave!" And he pecked me on the lips and walked out. I would miss that big brown cock with the U-bend. And his gym physique. And his pert peachy bum. And his plump lips. I nearly changed my mind and decided to embark on an affair. BUT NO, I had to be strong.

PING! My pornographic thoughts were disturbed by a text.

BILLY: I'm back in England.

I dropped my phone. Not because it slipped from my hand. But from the shock.

Billy's back (The next day)

TULLENE: What do you mean you never replied?

ME: Exactly that. I didn't reply.

TULLENE: Why not?

ME: I don't know.

TULLENE: I think you're stupid.

*ME: *sends shocked face emoji**

TULLENE: Some people don't even get the chance of love once in their life. You've had two men you've felt connected to on a deep level and you've chosen to ignore one of them.

ME: Well, one of them is dead so no prizes for guessing which one you're talking about.

*TULLENE: *sends shocked face emoji**

ME: Oh, as if you're shocked by anything I say anymore.

TULLENE: This is awkward.

Just because I could now joke about Travis, didn't mean I was over my grief. But humour always has been, and always will be, my coping mechanism. I don't think we ever get over the pain of losing a loved one. We just find ways of living with the grief and heartache to make life more bearable.

ME: What if he's back in England with Arthur?

TULLENE: And what if he isn't?

I hate it when Tullene has an answer for everything.

ME: So what do you think I should do?

TULLENE: Do you want to see him again?

ME: I guess so.

TULLENE: Then don't waste time. Losing Travis made us realise life is short remember. And he wouldn't want you to waste another 20 years with a different bloke!!

She had me there. Before Travis had finally gotten his act together and taken me on a date, Billy had come along and made me forget all about Travis. But then Billy fucked off to the other side of the world and then Travis finally took action. Now I no longer had Travis, Billy had arrived back in my life. It was obviously fate and I knew I would have been stupid to ignore the hand of fate any longer.

ME: Yay! Welcome home.

BILLY: Delayed reaction.

Glad to see he still possessed his sense of humour and sarcastic tones. And he still gave me a little trouser tremble everytime I thought of him or when I saw his name pop up on my phone screen.

ME: Get over it.

BILLY: Still as pleasant as ever I see.

ME: It's why you're attracted to me.

BILLY: Who says I'm attracted to you?

ME: I see the way you look at me with your tongue hanging out.

BILLY: I don't drink enough water. Perhaps I was just thirsty.

ME: Yeah. Thirsty for me.

I was so happy how we just slipped straight back into our banter filled conversation. Two years may have passed but it felt as though no time had passed at all. And still no mention of the elephant in the room. ARTHUR.

ME: You smuggled any fit kiwis into the country with you? In your suitcase?

Subtle, I thought. But it hadn't been subtle enough for Billy.

BILLY: If that's your way of asking about Arthur, then let me clarify things. He's a bastard and I left him where he belongs.

My eyes widened. Of course, I was desperate to get all the gossip and juicy details. But I also couldn't help feeling elated that Billy was obviously a single man. But I decided I shouldn't take that for granted. I decided to get clarity and confirmation of my assumption.

ME: Oh that's a shame.

BILLY: Don't pretend you're disappointed for me.

ME: Okay. I won't. But I am sorry if you got hurt.

BILLY: Thank you.

ME: So no other special person in your life?

BILLY: Give me a chance. I only landed back in London last night.

ME: Oh I see. What time did your flight land?

BILLY: 22:30.

I checked the time of his text message to me, informing me he was back. 22:31. He messaged me as soon as his plane landed. That must mean something.

BILLY: Let's not beat around the bush here Mark. Yes, I'm single. No, there's absolutely nobody in my life that I have a romantic connection with. And yes, I want to see you again now I'm back. And potentially pick up from where we left off two years ago.

I wanted clarity and confirmation. And there was no doubting or denying it- I had it, in black and white, right in front of my face on a phone screen.

ME: I'm sorry. I'm taken. About to get married.

I couldn't resist the joke. I had to keep him on his toes. But when radio silence ensued for two whole minutes, I thought better of it.

ME: Only joking!

BILLY: You cunt!

ME: That's why you love me.

BILLY: I want to take you on a walk. Just the two of us.

ME: You mean on a date?

BILLY: If that's what you want to call it.

CHAPTER 27

The date- if that's what you want to call it (June 2021)

It was a week or so before Billy finally took me on our walking date. But sorry, I shouldn't call it a date. Unless that's what you want to call it. I thought it was a rather funny way of wording things so, of course, Tullene and I dissected and analysed the statement during one of our morning conference calls.

"Is it a date or not?" Tullene was as confused as I was.

"Well yes, I'm sure it is."

"So why didn't he just say the word?"

"Maybe he got hurt with Arthur and is trying to protect himself," I offered.

"By not using the word date?"

I shrugged.

"Because the emission of that word is hardly going to stop you from getting hurt again."

"I'm just pleased he's back to be honest. WITHOUT Arthur. And that he's asked me on a..." Tullene quickly interrupted me.

"...NOT a date."

"Okay, okay. A lovely romantic walk in the Surrey Hills."

"That sounds like a date to me."

"I know that. And you know that. And I'm sure Billy does really."

"Then just tell him to call it a date."

Tullene began being deliberately provocative. So I ended the call abruptly. Not because I was being rude but because I had spotted a text from Billy pop up, that I desperately wanted to read.

BILLY: I've heard we're going to see some Belted Galloways on this walk. A hybrid variety. Of sheep and cow.

ME: Oh fuck off.

For those of you who think I have Tourette's; that was a private joke. Cast your minds back to the first time I ever met Billy back in 2016- he played a trick on me involving Belted Galloways, telling me they were a hybrid of two different farm animals. Not calling myself gullible but I fell for it. And here he was, still reminding me of it five years later.

I arrived at Gomshall- that's a beautiful little village in the Surrey Hills, in case you weren't aware. Getting out of my car to put on my walking boots, I saw Billy was already on the corner waiting for me.

"You're eager!" I shouted over as he approached to join me. "You must be really keen to see me."

"Don't read too much into that. I forgot it was school holidays so there was no rush hour."

OUCH! I had to get re-accustomed to his acerbic comebacks after a two year hiatus.

It hadn't escaped me that he had picked Gomshall for our non-date walk. Gomshall was the first walk I ever led and the first time we met. A romantic gesture? Or a complete coincidence? I chose to believe the former.

We walked. We talked. We held hands. We'd both experienced quite a bit of pain and trauma over the last couple of years. Travis dying. My breakdown. And it transpired that Arthur had been abusive and punched Billy during some arguments. I used the opportunity to show him I cared and squeezed his hand. He didn't let go and we continued through the woods, attached by our phalanges.

As we crossed into the next field, still holding on tight to one another, I spotted some cattle. Now, I've been a countryside walker for years now but cows still make me nervous. I've got an irrational fear that they're going to trample on me.

"Oh look!" Billy chirped up. "Here's your mates!" He took great delight at pointing out the large farm animals.

"Let's hurry up through this field!" I said, quickening my pace. But Billy refused to play ball and deliberately went slower with his walk.

"Can you see how they've got sheep faces and cow bodies?" Billy still hadn't got sick of that joke.

Feeling my heart beat begin to accelerate, I spotted a dog in the distance. Off the lead.

"There's a dog over there. And it's off the lead," I informed my walking companion.

"Oh yes. And there's it's owner. How unusual for a dog walker to be out walking their dog in the Surrey Hills." Now was not the time for Billy's sarcastic wit.

"Yes. But it's running about. It's scaring the cows. I can see them starting to move faster towards us. What if we get stampeded?" Yes, I'm irrational.

"Then I'll make sure that your obituary states that you were killed by hybrid cattle!" But I didn't have time for a witty comeback. The cows were moving at a much quicker pace. In OUR direction. My fight or flight instinct kicked in and I turned on my heels, pulled my hand from Billy's grip and started running in the opposite direction.

Billy didn't move from his spot. He'd obviously decided he liked the front row seats he had to the spectacle that was unravelling in front of his eyes. I let out an almighty scream as the cows drew closer. I decided that I couldn't escape them so I jumped onto a fence. PHEW! I felt calm as I saw the cows gracefully pass me and not stampede into the fence I was resting on. I saw Billy chuckling as he made his way towards me. I stuck two fingers up to indicate I didn't appreciate his laughing at me.

But karma is a bitch. Mummy Morgan always taught me it was very rude to do the 'V' sign. The action of said hand gesture caused me to lose my balance and I fell backwards off the fence I was sitting on.

SPLAT! I landed face down in a massive pile of cow pat. I was gagging at the smell, kicking and screaming. I couldn't get up.

"HELP ME! GET ME OUT!" I bellowed as I wallowed and splashed about in the brown-green goo. Billy arrived, laughing.

"I don't know what you think is so funny about this situation!" I yelled.

His response:

"You were made for me."

That stopped me in my tracks. I mean, not that I could get up at that moment anyway. I was stuck in cow shit.

CHAPTER 28

A proposal in Paris: Part One (July 2022)

Over a year of being re-united with Billy and I'd never known love like it before. Yes, I did just quote song lyrics. But I was lonely never more after Billy came into my life. Whoops, I did it again. I promise I won't do anymore.

To celebrate our one year anniversary, I decided to book us a romantic trip to Paris. I'd always wanted to go and to travel there by Eurostar. I was into my forties and I'd never graced the wheels of the infamous London to Paris train.

"I'm going to propose to Billy whilst we're in Paris." The room went silent. Well, it did after Tullene spat her prosecco out. And after Buttplug had slammed her vodka and tonic down on the coaster. Once my two friends had performed those actions, you could have heard a pin drop.

"Well say something." I ushered them.

They shared a look between themselves. It's quite hard to describe said glance but it was a mixture of bewilderment, happiness and total shock.

"But all you've ever wanted to do is shag. You always said settling down is for twats." Sometimes I wish Tullene didn't have the memory of an elephant. You can always rely on her to remind you of words from the past.

"People change. I've changed. I can't imagine my life without Billy now and I want to commit."

Buttplug hadn't managed to say anything. She was still catching flies. But I did catch a glimpse, a glimmer, of a tear in her eye.

"Do close your mouth Butt," I instructed her. "You don't want your tonsils to dry out, do you?"

She pulled top and bottom lips back together and then picked up her glass to take a swig of her V&T. Lifting the tumbler to the air, she offered her congratulations and said she was pleased for me.

"God. Don't tempt fate," I worried, "he hasn't said yes yet."

"He will."

Arriving at St Pancras station early one Saturday morning, I couldn't contain my excitement about going on the Eurostar for the first time in my life. I'm a bit of a train geek. I don't know why, I just love them- tubes, trains, whatever. I've even got the London Underground bed set. Billy always takes the piss out of me for it.

As we approached the passport queue, I started tugging at Billy's sleeve like an impatient child.

"Can you get the passports out?"

"There's still ten people ahead of us."

Billy has this really annoying habit of not taking the passports out of his bag until the last minute. But it panics me. I like to have them gripped tightly in my paws as soon as I join the line. Even if there are a hundred people in front.

And yes, Billy does control both of our passports, not because he is controlling of me but because I forgot to pack them when we went to Spain last Christmas. And he's never let me live it down.

"Can you get them out now?"

"There's still five people ahead of us."

I swear he does it deliberately, just to wind me up. He can see that it makes me jittery and on edge. Yes, I think I might be on the spectrum.

As we boarded the Eurostar, I entered mega geek mode, taking selfies in front of our carriage, ensuring the name and logo were on full display behind me. Billy isn't big on social media but I personally like to document my life like a reality tv star.

Taking our seats, Billy became a gentleman and tried to take my bag from me to put it in the overhead lockers. I snatched it back from him. His eyes widened, gazing at me as though I'd lost the plot.

"You can't look in this bag whilst we're away!" I instructed.

"When do I ever go through your bag? I was just going to place it in the luggage rack."

"That's okay then."

"Why are you acting weird?" Billy demanded answers.

The real reason I didn't want him to look inside my bag was because I had all the accessories for my planned proposal. Well, when I say accessories, I just mean I had the ring and a 'Will you marry me?' greetings card, which came complete with a YES/NO tick box on the front. And I had every intention of making him fill it out as soon as I'd dropped down onto one knee.

Two hours later and we were on French soil. It always amazes me how you can step on a train in England and then be in another country when you step off it. I know it goes under the ocean but it still blows my mind. I can't actually think too much about the logistics and location of it. I've got an irrational fear that the sea is going to break through and cave in the tunnel.

Walking through Gard du Nord station, I smiled at a guard and gleefully shouted "Bonjour", in a rather dodgy London accent trying to adopt a European twang. Billy raised his eyebrows in my direction. He seems to do that a lot. But I was very proud of my attempt at speaking the local lingo.

"I'm practically native mate!"

"Oh yes, because you managed to say hello in a dodgy sounding accent."

I remember we didn't half do some walking whilst we were in Paris. We did something stupid like 45,000 steps and we were only there for three days. We walked to see the Eiffel Tower, holding hands, acting like a teenage couple on heat.

Arriving at the massive French landmark, I got a rush of emotion and became overwhelmed. To see this huge piece of engineering that is over a hundred years old is quite mind blowing. Anything I witness around the world, any of the seven wonders or famous landmarks, always amazes me as they are pieces of architecture or nature that I thought I might only ever see in books. So to see them in the flesh, with my own eyes, I think that is rather special. And to share it with someone you love. The man who told me I was made for him. I felt very lucky.

"Shall we go up it?" Billy enquired. We both clapped eyes on the queue and quickly changed our minds. It went on for miles, circling around in many loops.

"Fuck that!" I said and we both nodded in agreement.

"I'm glad to see your French is improving."

I gave him a playful punch on his chest. Instead of queuing for half a day to make it to the top of the tower, we decided that a nice meal in a café next to it would be the perfect solution. We could fill our guts but also get to admire the scenery at the same time.

Does anybody else always eat a Croque Monsieur when they visit France? It's my go to dish. It's basically a ham and cheese toastie BUT better. Billy is a little more adventurous than me and ate some snails. He gave me one to try.

As I chewed away on the French delicacy, I saw Billy smirking as he could clearly see I wasn't enjoying what was in my mouth. My eyebrows and facial expressions are far too revealing. This is why I'm not a good liar. To give you my food critique of what a snail tastes and feels like in your mouth; *Garlic is the overwhelming flavour but it feels like you are biting down on a tendon.*

Washing the taste away with a glass of French savvy b; yes darlings, no New Zealand for me. Not whilst I'm holidaying in another country. I do like to try other countries offerings when I'm away. It's only polite.

Tucking into my croque monsieur, I noticed Billy becoming a bit fidgety. This normally only happens when he gets nervous or needs to tell me something he doesn't think I'm going to react well to. I know the signs. My immediate thought was that he was getting ready to propose.

He better bloody not! Especially after all the planning I've gone to. And besides, I do not want to be proposed to whilst shoving a Croque Monsieur in my gob.

"There's something I need to tell you."

I swallowed hard. And took a sharp intake of breath to prepare myself. He continued.

"I've been told I'm needed to go on another two year secondment to New Zealand."

I didn't say a word. My face said it all. All that could be heard was the clattering of knives and forks. And the chitter chatter of numerous accents and dialects. I picked up my glass of French plonk and did something I rarely do with wine. I knocked it back in one go.

A proposal in Paris: Part Two (Still July 2022. And still the same day)

"I just need to go to the toilet." I stood up rather abruptly.

"You can't just leave in the middle of a conversation like this."

"Watch me!" I tossed my napkin onto my empty Croque Monsieur plate and stormed away to the WC. I didn't look back to gage Billy's facial expression. Mainly because I didn't want him to see mine, which involved wiping a tear away.

I locked myself in the cubicle, fighting back more tears. After a struggle with my pocket, I managed to pull out my mobile.

ME: Tullene.

That's our private signal if ever we need the other in an emergency situation. We send a text with just the other's name.

TULLENE: What's happened?

ME: Billy just announced he's being sent to New Zealand again. For two more years.

TULLENE: WHAT THE FUCK.

ME: I know. I'm floored.

TULLENE: Well is he going to refuse?

ME: I don't know.

TULLENE: What do you mean you don't know?

ME: Well, I stormed off from the table as soon as he told me.

TULLENE: Well get back to that table and discuss it like an adult. NOW!

ME: Yes boss.

I needed that text slap from Tullene. In that moment, I realised I'd been childish and I couldn't just walk away from a conversation I didn't like. Not with the man I wanted to marry. I rushed out of the cubicle and dashed back to the table. But the chair where Billy had been sat was empty. I surveyed the cute little Parisian café but he was nowhere to be seen. I hurried outside to the hustle and bustle of market sellers and tourists at the feet of the Eiffel Tower. But Billy was nowhere to be seen amongst them.

BASTARD! Although I couldn't really blame him I suppose. I did just stand up and storm off. I pressed call on Billy's contact and all I got was the international ring tone. No answer. And then I caught sight of him, clutching onto a dozen red roses. By this point, I had tears streaming down both sides of my face. I practically sprinted towards him. I just wanted to hug him. And squeeze him tight but I decided against it in that moment. I didn't want to flatten the flowers in the process.

"They better be for me!" I managed to say. The usual sarcastic reply came.

"No. They're for the waitress in that café we were just in." He smirked.

"I'm sorry I walked off."

"If you had let me finish, I was going to tell you that I've requested not to be sent away. And I've made the decision to quit if they refuse my request." It was all too much for me. I broke down in tears.

AGAIN. Tears of relief. Everybody was staring at us as I cried, the Eiffel Tower towering over us. Billy held me tight and kissed my forehead.

"I'm not going anywhere. I only wanna be with you," he said in a very reassuring voice. A tone he doesn't often adopt with me but I think he realised sarcasm wasn't appropriate in this situation.

"No-one has ever bought me flowers before." And that was true. I had got to middle age without anyone ever giving me a bunch. The only bunch I'd ever been given was haemorrhoids; Genetically, from my mother. Oh my god, I can't believe I just called myself middle aged. Or that I just told you all that I have piles.

The evening of the proposal arrived and I was as nervous as a dormouse. Getting ready for the evening, I nearly gave my secret away. I blame the nerves.

"Why are you bringing a rucksack to dinner?" Billy quizzically asked.

"I just need it." I snapped back.

And I did. My equipment for the main event wouldn't fit in my pocket. I had the proposal card, the ring box and a pen. The latter of which I couldn't find in my bag.

"I need a pen!" I hadn't meant to say that out loud.

"What do you need a pen for dinner for?"

"I just do!" Billy performed an action he often adopts with me- the raising of his eyebrows.

"Why are you acting weird? Here's a pen." He handed me a hotel branded biro from the desk and I popped it in my bag.

As soon as we'd eaten, I embarked on part one of my plan which was to walk us up to the Sacre Coeur, which is where I planned for the actual proposal to take place. But having never been to this tourist hot spot, I didn't know just how high up it was or how many steps it takes to reach the top.

Halfway up, gasping for breath, I gripped the hand rail, deciding in that moment that I must give up smoking.

"Whose idea was it to come up here?" I managed to say between catching my breath.

"It was yours!" Billy took great pleasure in reminding me of the fact.

Reaching the top, I was in awe of how beautiful this church building was. And the view from the top… You can see all across Paris and as it was time for the sun to set, it made it even more beautiful. I couldn't believe how perfect the setting was for someone to pop the question. Stunning. I was speechless for once. Having never been to the Sacre Coeur before, I had taken a risk and relied on google to tell me the best place to propose in Paris. And this was one time my search engine didn't tell me I had cancer.

We strolled around, hand in hand, taking in the beauty that surrounded us. It was extremely busy, jam packed with hordes of sightseers. I suddenly got a pang of nerves. I didn't want a big audience for my marriage proposal. I know I'm a massive extrovert but this was one occasion I became rather introverted. It was starting to get dark at this point and the moon had taken the place of the sun. And Billy's urinary bladder had sent messages to his brain.

"We should go soon. I need a wee."

"NO!" I shouted. Witnessing how my overzealous tone had taken Billy aback, I took a deep breath. "Not yet."

"Right…"

It had to be there and then. I couldn't delay it any longer. Not unless I wanted Billy to piss himself whilst I was down on one knee. I sat him on a bench and went down on one knee.

"What are you doing?" He sounded bemused. "Have you got a cramp?"

I rummaged through my bag and handed him the card:

Will you Marry me?

Yes

No

"So this is why you wanted a pen!"

I placed the pen into his hand.

"You need to answer by placing a tick in the corresponding box," I informed him.

"You haven't even asked me anything."

FUCK. He was right. I was so nervous and my heart beating incredibly fast, I had forgotten to actually say the words and ask the question.

"Will you marry me Billy?"

Billy, being Billy, couldn't resist a practical joke, even in this serious moment and pretended to tick no. I playfully punched his arm and then he ticked yes. Who says violence doesn't get you what you want?

"Of course I will. I can't be in this life without you now."

I cried. The tears arrived like a tropical storm. Taking the ring from the box, I placed it on his finger and he kissed me.

"You can get up now." It hadn't even dawned on me that I was still down on one knee. It was the nerves. I wasn't thinking straight. Placing a hand on Billy's knee, I attempted to stand but my leg had gone to sleep.

"I can't." I'd been down for too long.

"Let me help you up old man." And Billy pulled me up and held me close.

"I love you to the end of the earth."

"And back."

The Final Chapter (March 2023)

As I sit writing in what I've come to call my undateable gay diary, I hope it's the last entry I will have to make as a single, so-called, *UNDATEABLE GAY.* When I look back, I can't believe how many frogs I encountered before finally bagging my prince.

Billy and I are about to marry and I intend to keep this one for life. No one night fling. No heart attacks during sex. He's my one for life. I can feel it.

I might start a new diary and call it *THE DATEABLE GAY,* or how about *THE MARRIED GAY.* Who knows what the future holds?

I've learnt to expect the unexpected over the years. Grab on to each moment as they happen and embrace them. Enjoy the experience. Hold your loved ones tight. Tell them you love them, even when they drive you mad. (*Tullene. Mummy Morgan. Buttplug. Billy.)*

And the biggest piece of advice I could ever give someone. Have great sex. And even if it can't always be great, just enjoy it. It releases endorphins after all, which are good for you. One of my friends who's a doctor told me, so it must be true.

Anyway, I'm off to walk down the aisle now. I've got the dream wedding I've always talked about; the one I described and talked about when I appeared on 'First Dates' on Channel 4 all those years ago…

I'm walking down the aisle to 'How will I know' by the legend that is Whitney. There's a glitterball hanging from the ceiling. And the priest will arrive from underneath the pulpit, spinning on a revolving platform from a hole underground. Very camp and dramatic. But did you really expect anything less?

Tullene and Buttplug are doubling up as bridesmaids and best women. Wish me luck with these two organising the day. I was sensible and gave Buttplug the job of looking after the rings. She's less likely to lose them.

I don't often pray but I'm here asking God for a favour…

Please don't let this one die on me!

THE END?...

ALSO BY MARK DAVID WOOLLARD

THE UNDATABLE GAY

Think you're unlucky in love ?

You know nothing of dating misery until you've delved into the world of the undatable gay

Mark Morgan just can't catch a break.

As he documents his struggles through the dating minefield of the gay world, Mark tries to find the answer to the eternal question:

does Mr Right truly exist?

With his best friend and fag hag, Tullene for support and a bottle of Savvy B (or 6), he battles his way through failed date after date. And ponders many a profound question:

How much savvy B is too much?

Will he ever be able to bottom?

Should you wear Ugg boots on a first date?

Can you find love in a gay sauna?

One man keeps popping up (pardon the pun) like a proverbial bad penny, but will Mark ever bag Travis.

Or should he leave him where he found him- in his late teens on a dance floor in G-A-Y?

DOWNLOAD THE FIRST BOOK IN THE UNDATABLE GAY'S ADVENTURES

Printed in Great Britain
by Amazon

42592184R00096